Best Recipes

hardie grant books

MELBOURNE · LONDON

First published in 2009
This edition published in 2010 by
Hardie Grant Books
85 High Street
Prahran, Victoria 3181, Australia
www.hardiegrant.com.au

Copyright © Hardie Grant Books 2009
Copyright photography (food) © Ian Hofstetter 2007
Photography on page 10: istockphoto.com
Photography on page 73: Ellie Smith

Cataloguing-in-Publication Data is available from
the National Library of Australia.

The Biggest Loser Best Recipes
ISBN 978 1 74066 884 2

Colour reproduction by Splitting Image Colour Studio
Printed and bound in China by C & C Offset Printing

10 9 8 7 6 5 4 3 2

NUTRITIONAL CONSULTANT
Dr Clare Collins,
PhD, BSc, Dip Nut&Diet,
Dip Clin Epi, AdvAPD, FDAA

COVER DESIGN
saso content & design pty ltd

TEXT DESIGN
Ellie Exarchos

FOOD PHOTOGRAPHY
Ian Hoftstetter

FOOD STYLING
Katy Holder
Jane Collins

FOOD PROPS
Alfresco Emporium
David Edmonds
MUD Australia
Villa Homewares

TEXT LAYOUT
Pauline Haas,
bluerinse setting

Contents

Introduction

Getting the energy equation right

When you look at the hard cold facts of weight loss, it comes down to these two words: energy balance. Calories 'in' must equal calories 'out' – right? Well, yes … and also no.

Everyone knows that the energy balance equation sounds very simple, in theory. The trouble is that there are a whole host of factors that can quietly sabotage the energy balance equation and your efforts to manage your weight. These saboteurs work subtly to push *up* your consumption of 'calories in' so that they exceed the number of calories you want.

Then there are the saboteurs that unremittingly get in the way of you burning more of those 'calories out'. They act as barriers to you being more active and push *down* your total daily physical activity so that you use fewer calories than you'd planned.

If this continues consistently over time, your energy equation tilts out of balance, your weight starts to creep up, and you are left wondering 'what happened?!' The reality is that you have may have unconsciously fallen into a pattern of energy *imbalance*.

'I was overweight because of bad management: I badly managed my body, my food, my activity and my lifestyle. In changing that, I learnt to appreciate and control myself, to live life rather than just be alive, and to see my health and body as more important assets than the house.'
Adro Sarnelli, Series One Winner

'Energy in' sabotage factors include:

- large portions
- oversized dinner plates
- skipping breakfast
- excessive snacking
- always feeling hungry
- drinks full of hidden calories
- multi-bags of snacks
- supermarkets with a large range of products
- big grocery trolleys
- takeaway and fried food
- eating out
- all-you-can-eat buffets
- food advertising
- eating in front of the TV.

'I don't eat junk food or chips anymore, but of course I still sometimes crave these foods, so my strategy is to be prepared. I always carry a supply of nuts and tuna around so that if I get caught out and about, I have healthy food I can snack on. I also always try to eat every three hours so that I don't reach that starving stage when I know I'd reach for the first bad thing I see.'
Cat White, Series One

The bottom line is that we cross paths with too many tasty, calorie-rich foods that are heavily advertised and easily available. Becoming more conscious of these influences is the first step to changing habits that undermine your weight-loss efforts.

'Energy out' sabotage factors include:

- lack of time
- lack of energy
- not making physical activity a priority
- financial constraints
- not feeling fit enough to even start being active
- not having an exercise companion
- lack of motivation
- lack of confidence
- not liking exercise.

*'Remember to look at your weight loss in small numbers. I had to lose
70 kilograms and I thought, there is no way I can do this. But then I set
my weight-loss goals in 10-kilogram brackets. Once I lost the first
10 kilos, it was goal achieved and on to the next 10 kilos! Take on a
"can do" attitude because you CAN do it, you really can – I did!'*
Artie Rocke, Series One

The key to increasing your physical activity is making a commitment to setting aside the time, and finding activities that you can learn to enjoy enough that they become a habit. Getting started on the path to a more physically active life is hard work, as is staying motivated to the point where you feel fit enough to override distractions such as the TV or the couch. But it's worth it!

Beating your weight-loss saboteurs

The good news is that the more you learn to recognise factors that sabotage your weight-loss plan, the faster you will learn to arm yourself with counter-strategies. You can build these into a personalised plan of counter-attack, so that you are the winner in the long-term war on unhealthy weight gain.

SABOTEURS	COUNTER-TACTICS
Large portions	• Share a meal • Order an entrée for your main meal • Avoid up-sizing • Use a portion control monitor (such as the Template System, www.templatesystem.com.au) • Make sure half to three-quarters of your plate comprises vegetables or salad • Use a half cup measure to serve out each portion • Use sandwich bread rather than toasting bread (which is often thicker)
Oversized dinner plates	• Use small, entrée-sized plates • Use smaller cups and bowls
Skipping breakfast	• Set the breakfast table the night before • Pack your breakfast and take it to work • Keep a store of breakfast cereal at work • Try eating dinner earlier so you are hungry in the morning
Excessive snacking	• Plan ahead by purchasing low-calorie, low-fat snacks (fewer than 100 calories or 400 kilojoules per serve) • Buy in-season fruit and take a piece with you wherever you go • Suggest your workplace replace the biscuit barrel with free fruit • Try low-fat yoghurt and berries • Pack snacks for the day into your bag so they are on hand when the munchies hit
Always feeling hungry	• Try to include a small to medium serve of lean protein at each meal such as skim milk or yoghurt, egg white, chicken, fish or lean red meat • Increase your daily serves and variety of fruit and vegetables • Add vegetables to all main dishes to lower the energy density of each meal
Drinks full of hidden calories	• Always carry a refillable water bottle • Switch to diet soft drink and cordials • Keep a water jug in the fridge • Always put a water jug on the table • When you are thirsty, reach for water or a diet drink first • Alternate alcoholic drinks with water or diet drinks • Limit fruit juice to 125 ml per day (or dilute it with water) • Avoid rounds or 'shouts' at the pub

SABOTEURS	COUNTER-TACTICS
Multi-bags of snacks	• Avoid multi-bags • Only purchase what you are 100 per cent sure you want to eat or are happy for your kids to consume • Stick to the smaller multi-bags available (for example, twelve serves rather than thirty serves) because bigger bags mean you will have more temptation or will have to say 'no' to the kids more often
Supermarkets with a large range of products	• Write a list based on the week's meals and resist impulse purchases • Go shopping after a meal when you are least hungry and less likely to be tempted • Stick to the outer aisles, which contain the fresh food
Big grocery trolleys	• Resist shopping until the trolley is full • Limit the number of times you go to the supermarket each week • Fill up with fruit, vegetables and breads first • Grab a basket when you only need a few items
Takeaway fast food	• Plan a week's meals ahead and make a grocery list to match so you don't get caught out by a bare pantry • Have a box of fruit and vegetables home delivered so you have a supply of fresh food to hand • Collect your favourite fast recipes in a folder for easy reference
Eating out	• Reduce the frequency • Choose the places you go carefully • Avoid going out in big groups where it's easy to over order
All-you-can-eat buffets	• Avoid buffets as they are not good value for your waistline
Food advertising	• Limit the number of TVs in your house • No TVs in bedrooms • Pre-record TV programs, especially for kids, so you can fast forward the ads • Monitor or limit internet usage and kids' magazines • Don't support fundraisers that target children with advertising • Have your say on advertising to kids at www.parentsjury.org.au

SABOTEURS	COUNTER-TACTICS
Eating in front of the TV	• Make it a house rule to turn off the TV during meals • Always eat at the table • Buy a tablecloth or placemats and always set the table • Have everyone eat meals together
Lack of time	• Order groceries online • Have fruit and vegetables home delivered • Put some tasty ten-minute meal recipes in a folder • Use the grocery list feature from the Biggest Loser Club online menus
Lack of energy	• Start with small efforts – every bit counts! • Begin with a gentle exercise program and work up to more energetic activities when your body is ready for it • Remember that being fitter will give you more energy in the long run
Not making physical activity a priority	• Use an exercise bike or treadmill while watching TV • Incorporate physical activity in family time
Financial constraints	• You don't have to join an expensive gym to get fit – walking around the block costs next to nothing! • Buy second-hand equipment
Lack of motivation	• Find a healthy lifestyle partner • Share healthy recipes with a friend • Commit to a regular walk with a neighbour • Persuade a workmate to lose weight with you • Join the Biggest Loser Club
Lack of confidence	• Start with small, achievable changes • Enlist the support of a family member or friend • Join a community weight-loss group for advice and encouragement
Not liking exercise	• Exercise often feels unpleasant when we push ourselves too hard, too early – start slow and build up as your fitness increases • Find an activity that will feel comfortable at your current fitness level – walking, light weights and some forms of yoga are good options to start with • Think outside the square – join a dance group or replant the garden. That counts as exercise too!

Winning tactics

There is even more good news! A group of successful losers have shown that it is possible to survive as a slimmer you, even in today's challenging environment. Thousands of people who have lost weight and kept it off for an average of five years are enrolled on the US National Weight Control Register. To be eligible, they must have lost a minimum of fifteen kilograms and kept it off for at least two years. The characteristics of these successful losers have been studied and reported so we now know a lot more about what it takes to keep excess weight off.

'Losing weight feels amazing. I don't know which is greater —
the physical joy or the joy of knowing that I beat a demon that has
controlled me since childhood. Either way, life is amazing now.'
Adro Sarnelli, Series One Winner

The key is making lifestyle changes you can live with for the rest of your life. Focusing your efforts on adopting healthy lifestyle habits that you can put into practice every day will yield the best long-term results, and become easier as time goes on. Here are some of the most common habits of successful losers:

- **Weigh yourself regularly at the same time every week.** This will let you track your progress consistently. Also use a diary to keep track of your body measurements because sometimes weight loss will show up on the tape measure before the scales.
- **Eat breakfast every day.** Eating a good breakfast will kickstart your metabolism and give you fuel to start the day. If you are too busy in the mornings, have breakfast at work. If you aren't usually hungry in the mornings, start with fruit or a smoothie and, over time, move to more substantial food such as toast, muesli or porridge.
- **Follow a low-fat diet.** Use the leanest meat you can afford, making sure to include chicken or fish a few times a week, as well as vegetarian meals using lentils, chickpeas or kidney beans. Use low-fat dairy products and low-fat cooking techniques (stir-fry, steam, grill), switch to wholegrain breads and cereals, and include lots of vegetables and fruit every day. One common factor among the National Weight Control Register members is a low-fat diet. Despite having used a range of different types of diets and

dieting approaches to lose weight initially, once they reached their goal weight they switched to a low-fat maintenance diet that allows a greater range of food and more satisfying serves than other diet approaches.

- **Self-monitor your 'calories in' and 'calories out'.** Make a regular or even an intermittent habit of noting your what you consume and how much physical activity you do on a usual day. Use a paper journal or an online diary, like the one used by the Biggest Loser Club. If you need more help, visit an Accredited Practising Dietitian (APD); you can find your nearest APD at www.daa.asn.au.
- **Aim for an average of at least sixty minutes of physical activity every day.** If you can't fit in a one-hour block, grab bites of activity whenever you can – ten minutes here and there soon adds up, and you can use the weekend to get ahead or catch up.
- **Watch total calories on weekends as well as weekdays.** Avoid the Monday-to-Friday diet trap. Staying consistent on the weekend means you don't spend all week trying to undo the damage wreaked by two days of indulgence.
- **Eat fast food, takeaways or fried food only occasionally.** Enjoy the occasional meal 'off', but don't have the whole day off.
- **Jump on small rebounds in weight sooner rather than later.** If you do have a bad day or a bad patch, start again on your healthy eating and activity plan as soon as possible. Tackling a rebound of a couple of kilograms is much easier than waiting until the rebound has skyrocketed to twenty or thirty kilograms.
- **Be realistic about the body weight you can maintain successfully in the long run.** You will discover this by adopting the healthy habits you feel you can live with and put into practice most of the time, and seeing what weight this takes you to.

'I had to confront my own personal demons before I could lose weight. Finding the thing that makes you overeat, choose unhealthy food and not exercise can be difficult but, if you're like me, you have to deal with the WHY first.'
Shane Giles, Series One

Create a supportive environment for yourself

Sometimes family and friends may be threatened by your weight loss program, especially if they find managing their own weight a struggle. Alternatively, they may have been nagging you for years to do something about your weight and lifestyle, and now suddenly you've made some major changes and become the 'diet police' at home or work.

Even though it can be a struggle at first, try to elicit the support of your family, friends, neighbours and even work colleagues. It's vital to surround yourself with positive and encouraging influences to help you maintain your strategies for weight loss and a long-term healthy lifestyle. They may even be inspired to make some positive changes themselves!

'Learn to love and accept yourself for who you are. Only then will you succeed at anything you want to do. When the time is right for you, it will be like a light bulb going on. Don't be afraid to ask for help and don't surround yourself with negative people.'

Jo Cowling, Series One

Why exercise?

If you've seen the show, you know how hard the contestants work to get fit. Yes, it's hard work but, as the Biggest Losers will confirm, the results are well worth it. Every contestant felt an improved sense of health and wellbeing, and a renewed energy and passion for their lives, and so will you. Of course, you're not expected to work out 5 hours a day like the contestants on *The Biggest Loser* – that was a competition. You have work commitments, family, kids to look after, friends to catch up with and a life to live, so that's just not feasible. You need something that you can maintain – and enjoy – for the rest of your life, and this exercise plan will set you up for that.

By regularly exercising, you're committing to *your* health and wellbeing. We invest time and energy into managing our finances, our families and our property – we also need to make that investment for ourselves. The best way to create more time for your future – that is, a longer life – is to invest in yourself and your health *now*. If this isn't a good enough reason to put down the remote and get moving, what is?

Maybe you didn't like sport at school and haven't played any since – that's okay. Developing a healthy lifestyle doesn't mean you have to suddenly become a keen footballer or runner. First, all you need to do is get moving, then, knowing that exercise will make you look and feel better, why not try it? Experience the adrenalin rush of a decent workout, the buzz afterwards at your sense of achievement and the gradual changes as your fitness levels improve and your weight reduces. This could be yours before you've even had breakfast!

The benefits

A common mistake people make is to assume that by not seeing instant weight-loss, no progress is being made. Whatever your reasons for exercising there are numerous advantages to getting moving regularly. Weight-loss is one benefit; here are some others:

- improved sleep
- improved libido
- increased metabolism
- higher self-esteem
- reduced risk of cardiovascular disease, stroke, diabetes and osteoporosis
- increased energy
- reduced likelihood of depression and its effects
- improved lung capacity
- healthy blood pressure.

Exercise will have a positive effect on your daily life. The fitter you become, the easier life gets – you'll have more energy for everything from picking up the shopping, dancing the night away or chasing your grandkids. If you exercise regularly, you will:

- feel stronger and be stronger
- be less stressed
- breathe more easily (and be less likely to snore)
- fit into your favourite clothes
- keep up with your kids
- receive compliments about how great you look
- be more flexible and have better balance.

'I always knew it would be great to fit into nice clothes when I had lost weight, but I didn't realise that was just the tip of the iceberg. Now I don't creak when I get out of bed and I never groan when climbing stairs. My moods are constant and my energy levels are just through the roof. I still don't love training but I love the wonderful feeling I get when I have finished a tough session. I can honestly say that I feel younger than I have in years.' *Kristie Dignam, Series One*

Dietary Guidelines for Australians* and what each means for weight reduction and healthy eating

The Dietary Guidelines for Australian Adults provide broad food and nutrition recommendations designed to improve the health of adults. *The Biggest Loser Best Recipes* has taken these recommendations on board and brings you a selection of tasty recipes that fit with good taste, good health and the Guidelines.

Enjoy a wide variety of nutritious foods:

- Eat plenty of vegetables, legumes and fruits
- Eat plenty of cereals (including breads, rice, pasta and noodles), preferably wholegrain
- Include lean meat, fish, poultry and/or alternatives
- Include milks, yoghurts, cheeses and/or alternatives. Reduced-fat varieties should be chosen, where possible
- Drink plenty of water.

And take care to:

- Limit saturated fat and moderate total fat intake
- Choose foods low in salt
- Limit your alcohol intake if you choose to drink
- Consume only moderate amounts of sugars and foods containing added sugars.

Prevent weight gain: be physically active and eat according to your energy needs

Care for your food: prepare and store it safely

Encourage and support breastfeeding

* Australian Government Department of Health and Ageing

To help translate the Dietary Guidelines into food choices, Australia has a National Food Selection Guide called the Australian Guide to Healthy Eating (AGHE). The AGHE separates foods into two groups. The 'Core' foods are regarded as essential for health and the fats and 'Non-core' or 'extra' foods are higher in calories but tend to be lower in essential nutrients. The Core foods are presented in the shape of a plate divided into sections. Each section symbolises the proportion each Core food group would ideally provide in our overall food intake.

The Core food groups are:

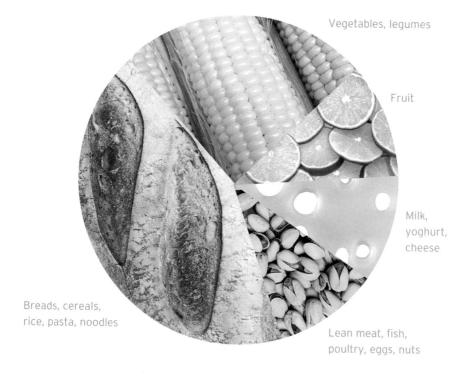

Vegetables, legumes

Fruit

Milk, yoghurt, cheese

Breads, cereals, rice, pasta, noodles

Lean meat, fish, poultry, eggs, nuts

Choose the following sometimes or in small amounts:
Biscuits, fizzy drinks, pies, hot chips, chocolate, ice cream and unsaturated fats.

Food serves for weight-loss from the AGHE

	Breads and Cereals	Vegetables and Legumes	Fruit	Dairy Foods	Meat and Alternatives	Non-core Extras
MEN	4-7	5-8	2-4	2-4	1-2	0-3
WOMEN	3-6	4-7	2-3	2-3	1-1½	0-2

The number of serves that are right for your individual weight-loss plan will depend on how physically active you are, your current body weight and how fast you want to lose weight. The number of Non-core extras also depends on your age, weight and degree of physical activity.

What is a standard portion size (as defined in AGHE)?

1. Bread, cereals, rice, pasta, noodles

This group includes grains such as wheat, rye, oats, rice, barley, millet and corn, and foods such as breakfast cereals, bread, pasta and noodles. It provides B vitamins, thiamin, riboflavin and niacin, and folate as well as carbohydrate and fibre. Wholemeal, wholegrain and high-fibre varieties provide more fibre than refined versions.

A serve is equivalent to:
- 2 slices of bread
- 1 medium bread roll
- 1 cup cooked rice, pasta, noodles
- 1 cup porridge
- 1⅓ cups breakfast cereal flakes
- ½ cup muesli.

2. Vegetables and legumes

Vegetables and legumes come from plants. They can be leaves, roots, tubers, flowers, stems, seeds or shoots and provide vitamins (beta-carotene, C, B, folate), minerals (zinc, iron, potassium), dietary fibre and carbohydrate.

A serve is equivalent to:

- ½ cup or 75 g cooked vegetables
- ½ cup or 75 g cooked legumes (dried beans, peas or lentils)
- 1 cup salad vegetables
- 1 medium potato.

3. Fruit

Fruit comes from the flower of the plant and contains the seeds. Natural fruit sugars gives it its sweetness. Fruit is a good source of vitamins (vitamin C, B and folate).

A serve is equivalent to:

- 150 g of fresh fruit
- 1 medium piece; e.g. apple, banana, orange, pear
- 2 small pieces; e.g. apricots, kiwi fruit, plums
- 1 cup diced pieces or canned fruit
- ½ cup (125 ml) juice
- dried fruit; e.g. 4 dried apricot halves
- 1½ tablespoons sultanas.

4. Milk, yoghurt, cheese

Dairy products are derived from milk and provide an excellent source of calcium. To achieve a healthy weight choose the skimmed and low-fat varieties.

A serve is equivalent to:

- 250 ml (1 cup) fresh, long-life or reconstituted dried milk
- ½ cup evaporated milk
- 40 g (2 slices) cheese
- 200 g (1 small carton) yoghurt
- 250 ml (1 cup) custard.

5. Meat, fish, poultry and alternatives

This group includes meat, fish, poultry, eggs, nuts and seeds. They are a good source of protein, niacin and vitamin B12 and an excellent source of the minerals iron and zinc. Legumes are included again because they are high in protein.

A serve is equivalent to:

- 65–100 g cooked meat, chicken; e.g. $1/2$ cup lean mince, 2 small chops or 2 slices roast meat
- $1/2$ cup cooked (dried) beans, lentils, chickpeas, split peas, or canned beans
- 80–120 g cooked fish fillet
- 2 small eggs
- $1/3$ cup peanuts or almonds
- $1/4$ cup sunflower seeds or sesame seeds.

6. Non-core or 'extra' foods

Foods that don't fit into the Core foods are not essential to the body's needs. They may add to food enjoyment but add large amounts of calories (kilojoules). The amount of 'extras' depends on you weight-loss goals, your physical activity levels and your age.

A serve is equivalent to the amount of food that provides 150 calories (600 kJ):

- 1 can (375 ml) soft drink
- (60 g) meat pie or pastie
- 12 (60 g) hot chips
- $1/2$ scoops (50 g scoop) ice cream
- 1 (40 g) doughnut
- 4 (35 g) plain sweet biscuits
- 1 fun size chocolate bar or a milk Freddo (25 g)
- 2 tablespoons (40 g) cream, mayonnaise
- 1 tablespoon (20 g) butter, margarine, oil
- 200 ml wine (2 standard drinks)*
- 60 ml spirits (2 standard drinks)*
- 600 ml light beer ($1/2$ standard drinks)*
- 400 ml regular beer ($1/2$ standard drinks).*

* Note about alcohol

The recommendations for maximum daily alcohol intake are 4 standard drinks a day for men and 2 standard drinks a day for women with at least two alcohol-free days each week. Drinking more alcohol than this will result in weight gain and increases the risk of damage to your health.

* Note about caffeine

Caffeine increases your pulse rate, breathing rate and the secretion of acid in your stomach and stimulates your gall bladder to contract. It can be helpful to still have some caffeine when you are losing weight because it does help to reduce your risk of gall stones. Large amounts can contribute to headaches, heart palpitations, stomach upsets and sleeping problems. Caffeine is broken down in the liver and while most adults can tolerate about 300 mg a day, some people will be more sensitive to its effects. To check out if you are hooked on caffeine, record how many of the following you usually have in a day. The caffeine content does vary depending on brand and how strongly it is made.

· 1 cup of tea	10–90 mg
· 1 cup of instant coffee	50–100 mg
· 1 cup of brewed coffee	100–150 mg
· 1 can cola-type drink	40–50 mg
· 1 cup hot chocolate	20–70 mg
· 30 g (fun size) chocolate bar	20 mg

NUTRIENT	GOOD FOOD SOURCES	FUNCTION IN THE BODY
Protein	You need between 0.8 to 1 g of protein per kilogram of body weight per day. Meat, fish, chicken, dairy products, legumes, nuts and seeds.	Made from building blocks, called amino acids, that are used to make and repair all cells in the body. Conserve muscles during weight-loss.
Fat	A low-fat diet has about 30% of the calories from fat and only 8–10% from saturated fat. Sunflower, safflower, canola or olive oils or margarines, nuts or seeds and avocado. Saturated fat comes from animal products such as meat and full-fat dairy products and butter.	Body fat insulates and protects the vital organs. Carries and stores the fat-soluble vitamins. Used in all cell membranes and to make chemicals essential to regulate body processes such as inflammation, blood clotting and immune function. To reduce your risk of gall stones you need to keep at least 20 g of healthy fats in your food intake each day.
Carbohydrate	Wholemeal and wholegrain bread and pasta products, breakfast cereal, brown rice, low-fat dairy products, fruit and vegetables, salad, legumes such as chickpeas, lentils, soy beans, baked beans, red kidney beans.	The preferred source of fuel for the body. Helps to conserve protein for the body.
Fibre	Aim for 30 g per day. Vegetables, salad, fruit, wholemeal and wholegrain bread and cereals, chickpeas, lentils, soy beans, baked beans, red kidney beans, psyllium husks, wheat bran or oat bran added to breakfast cereal.	A high-fibre diet helps to reduce the risk of constipation and gall stones in the short-term and diverticulitis and colon cancer in the long-term.

VITAMIN	GOOD FOOD SOURCES	FUNCTION IN THE BODY
Thiamin (Vitamin B1)	Wholemeal cereal grains, sesame seeds, soy beans and other dried beans and peas, wheatgerm fortified breakfast cereals, bread, Vegemite and Promite, watermelon, yeast and pork.	To metabolise carbohydrate and convert glucose into energy. Used in nerves, and to maintain muscles.
Riboflavin (Vitamin B2)	Milk, yoghurt, cheese, wholegrain breads and cereals, egg white, leafy green vegetables, mushrooms, Vegemite and Promite, meat, liver and kidney.	To release energy from food and supports healthy eyesight and skin.
Vitamin B3 (niacin)	Lean meats, milk, eggs, wholegrain breads and cereals, tuna, salmon, nuts, leafy green vegetables.	Needed to metabolise protein, fat, carbohydrate and alcohol and to produce energy. Helps to lower cholesterol, maintain healthy skin, nerves and digestive system.
Folic acid (folate)	Green leafy vegetables, legumes, seeds, liver, poultry, eggs, cereals and citrus fruits. Many cereal-based foods in Australia, such as bread and breakfast cereals, are fortified with folate.	To form red blood cells, which carry oxygen around the body. Development of a healthy baby in pregnant women. Used in DNA synthesis and cell growth. Women of child-bearing age or planning a pregnancy need a diet rich in folic acid and should consider taking supplements or eat fortified foods to reduce the risk of neural tube defects such as spina bifida in the baby.
Vitamin C	Fruit, especially citrus, pineapple, mango and pawpaw. Vegetables, especially capsicum, broccoli, Brussels sprouts, cabbage, spinach.	Used in making connective tissue and blood vessels. For healthy teeth, gums and bones. To help with iron absorption and in wound healing and fighting infection.
Beta-carotene (Vitamin A precursor)	Dark yellow and orange and dark green vegetables and fruit such as apricots, mango and rockmelon, carrots, sweet potato and pumpkin, spinach and broccoli.	Beta-carotene is converted to retinol in the intestine. Retinol is used to convert light to images sent to your brain as sight. Needed for normal growth, to help fight infections and can act as an antioxidant.
Vitamin D	Formed in the skin from sunlight. Oily fish, eggs, margarine, butter, cheese and fish oils.	Promotes strong bone development and helps with the absorption of calcium and phosphorus.

MINERAL	GOOD FOOD SOURCES	FUNCTION IN THE BODY
Zinc	Meat, chicken, fish, oysters, legumes, nuts, wholemeal and wholegrain products.	To help in wound healing, development of the immune system and other essential functions in the body, including taste and smell.
Iron	There are two types of iron. **Haem iron** – found in animal foods such as beef, chicken and fish and in liver and kidney. **Non-haem iron** – found in plant foods such as beans, nuts, lentils and leafy green vegetables. Vegetarian sources include iron-fortified breakfast cereals, flours and grains.	To make haemoglobin in red blood cells and prevent anaemia. Assists many enzymes needed in chemical reactions in the body. Vitamin C, meat and the cooking process boost iron absorption.
Calcium	Dairy foods, such as milk, cheese, yoghurt, canned salmon and sardines with bones, fortified soy milks, leafy green vegetables, such as broccoli, bok choy, Chinese cabbage and spinach, brazil nuts, almonds and sesame seed paste (tahini).	To make bones and teeth. For healthy nerves, regulating muscle contraction and relaxation, regulating heart function, blood clotting, nerve transmission and enzyme function.
Magnesium	Tofu, soy beans, nuts, seeds, lean meat, spinach, barley, wheatgerm, brown rice, avocado, bananas, peanut butter and peas.	Needed for enzymes that release energy in the body, to make new cells and for healthy heart and muscle contraction.

Household weights and measures

Teaspoons, tablespoons, cups

1 Australian metric teaspoon = 5 ml/5 g

1 Australian metric tablespoon = 20 ml/20 g

1 Australian metric cup = 250 ml

3 tablespoons = ¼ cup

4 tablespoons = ⅓ cup

Oven temperatures

OVEN TEMPERATURES	°C (CELSIUS)	°F (FAHRENHEIT)
Very slow	120	250
Slow	150	300
Moderately slow	160	325
Moderate	180	350
Moderately hot	190	375
Hot	200	400
Very hot	220-250	450-500

N.B. When using a fan-forced oven, decrease the oven temperature by 20°C (i.e. 180°C becomes 160°C in a fan-forced oven).

Breakfasts

Berry-mint smoothie

A wonderful refresher on hot summer days.

¼ cup frozen mixed berries

¾ cup strawberries, hulled

½ teaspoon honey

2 tablespoons low-fat natural yoghurt

½ cup unsweetened apple juice

¼ cup roughly chopped mint leaves

3 tablespoons rolled oats

5 ice cubes

mint leaves to garnish (optional)

- Place all ingredients in a blender and mix until smooth. Drink immediately.

Serves 1

Nutritional Analysis
per Serve

Total kJ: 869

Total calories: 209

Carbohydrates: 34.3 g

Protein: 7.5 g

Fat – total: 2.9 g

Fat – saturated: 0.8 g

Fibre: 5.9 g

Bircher muesli

A light and colourful breakfast. Add any combination of nuts and seeds.

1½ cups rolled oats

1½ cups water

1 apple, grated

¾ cup low-fat natural yoghurt

¼ cup roughly chopped walnuts

2 tablespoons honey

1 teaspoon ground cinnamon

2 tablespoons pepitas
  (pumpkin seed kernels)

- Soak the oats in the water overnight. Add remaining ingredients and mix well. Serve topped with seasonal fruit (or Stewed Apple and Rhubarb, page 54).

Serves 4

Nutritional Analysis
per Serve

Total kJ: 1356
Total calories: 325
Carbohydrates: 42 g
Protein: 9 g
Fat – total: 12 g
Fat – saturated: 1.8 g
Fibre: 4.3 g

Berry compote

Very quick to make, this fruity mix is delicious with porridge or on pancakes.

1 cup frozen mixed berries

¾ cup strawberries,
   hulled and quartered

¼ cup caster sugar

1 vanilla bean, split lengthwise

1 tablespoon water

- Place all ingredients in a small saucepan. Cook gently over a low heat for 10 minutes or until strawberries are tender. Serve hot or refrigerate once cooled.

Serves 8

Nutritional Analysis
per Serve

Total kJ: 198
Total calories: 48
Carbohydrates: 9.1 g
Protein: 1.6 g
Fat – total: 0.1 g
Fat – saturated: 0 g
Fibre: 2.1 g

Buckwheat pancakes

Buckwheat actually contains no wheat or gluten, so is great for coeliacs.

¾ cup buckwheat flour

¼ cup caster sugar

¼ teaspoon ground nutmeg

½ teaspoon baking powder

¼ cup low-fat milk

1 egg yolk

3 egg whites

olive oil spray

- Combine flour, sugar, nutmeg and baking powder in a large mixing bowl. Add milk and egg yolk and mix thoroughly.
- Whisk egg whites until fluffy and gently fold into the flour mixture, forming a smooth batter.
- Heat a frying pan over medium heat and spray lightly with oil. Pour the batter into a jug and pour enough batter into the pan to coat the bottom. Cook until small bubbles form on the surface, then flip over and cook for a further couple of minutes or until golden. Serve warm topped with fresh or stewed fruits (or Berry Compote, page 30).

Serves 4

Nutritional Analysis
per Serve

Total kJ: 731
Total calories: 175
Carbohydrates: 28.9 g
Protein: 11.5 g
Fat – total: 1.7 g
Fat – saturated: 0.6 g
Fibre: 0.3 g

Slow-roasted garlic mushrooms

Mushrooms are a valuable source of protein and B vitamins. This recipe uses flat mushrooms but any type will do.

600 g flat mushrooms, wiped and
   stalks removed
4 cloves garlic, thinly sliced
light olive oil spray
4 sprigs thyme
75 g rocket leaves, washed
4 slices sourdough bread

- Preheat oven to 180°C.
- Place mushrooms and garlic in a baking dish. Spray lightly with oil and toss to coat. Add thyme sprigs and cover with a lid or foil. Bake for 1 hour, tossing occasionally.
- Remove thyme and serve atop rocket leaves on unbuttered slices of toasted sourdough.

Serves 4

Nutritional Analysis
per Serve

Total kJ: 489
Total calories: 117
Carbohydrates: 11.2 g
Protein: 9.5 g
Fat – total: 3.4 g
Fat – saturated: 0.7 g
Fibre: 6.4 g

Avocado and fetta salsa

Delicious on toast as a quick breakfast. The salsa can also be added to egg whites to make a tasty omelette.

olive oil spray

2 red onions, finely diced

2 cloves garlic, finely sliced

2 ripe roma tomatoes, diced

1½ ripe avocados, cut into 2 cm pieces

2 tablespoons chopped oregano leaves

80 g low-fat fetta, crumbled

freshly ground black pepper

- Heat a large frying pan over a low heat and spray lightly with oil. Cook the onions and garlic gently for a few minutes until soft. Add the tomato, avocado and oregano and stir gently until warmed through. Add the fetta and allow to melt slightly. Season and serve warm.

Serves 4

Nutritional Analysis
per Serve

Total kJ: 1121

Total calories: 269

Carbohydrates: 4.5 g

Protein: 8.4 g

Fat – total: 23 g

Fat – saturated: 6.3 g

Fibre: 3.2 g

Italian omelette

A hearty and satisfying breakfast. For a vegetarian version, substitute a handful of chopped mushrooms for the ham.

olive oil spray

2 red onions, finely diced

2 cloves garlic, crushed

4 slices fat-free leg ham, chopped

4 eggs, lightly beaten

8 egg whites, lightly beaten

¼ cup skim milk

1 tablespoon grated reduced-fat
   cheddar cheese

1 tablespoon chopped oregano leaves

200 g reduced-fat ricotta

Nutritional Analysis
per Serve

Total kJ: 973
Total calories: 234
Carbohydrates: 4.4 g
Protein: 25.4 g
Fat – total: 12.7 g
Fat – saturated: 5.8 g
Fibre: 0.4 g

- Heat a small frying pan over a low heat and spray lightly with oil. Gently cook the onions, garlic and ham for a few minutes until onions soften.
- Combine eggs, egg whites, milk, cheese and oregano in a mixing bowl. Remove the onion mixture from the heat, allow to cool slightly, and fold into the eggs.
- Spray the frying pan lightly with a little more oil and pour a quarter of the mixture into the pan. Cook over a medium heat until it begins to set. Sprinkle 50 g of the ricotta over one half of the omelette and use a spatula to fold the other side over to cover. Cook for a further 5 minutes. Loosen the base and sides and gently slide out of the pan. Repeat with remaining mixture.

Serves 4

Scrambled eggs with smoked salmon

Salmon is a valuable source of essential fatty acids. This delicious breakfast takes just minutes to prepare.

olive oil spray

1 onion, finely diced

4 eggs

8 egg whites

8 slices smoked salmon, cut into
   1 cm strips

2 tablespoons chopped chives

4 slices sourdough bread

- Heat a large frying pan over a low-medium heat and spray lightly with oil. Add the onion and cook gently until soft.
- Beat the eggs and egg whites together and pour into the pan. Stir continuously for 3-5 minutes until cooked.
- Remove from heat and combine with the salmon and chives. Serve immediately on unbuttered slices of toasted sourdough.

Serves 4

Nutritional Analysis
per Serve

Total kJ: 998

Total calories: 240

Carbohydrates: 12.8 g

Protein: 27 g

Fat - total: 8.4 g

Fat - saturated: 2.2 g

Fibre: 1.9 g

Spanish-style baked eggs

This is an interesting twist on eggs for breakfast, with robust flavours.

2 red capsicums

olive oil spray

1 onion, finely sliced

2 cloves garlic, finely sliced

100 g baby spinach leaves

2 cups tomato passata

2 tablespoons capers, roughly chopped

10 pitted black olives, roughly chopped

1/3 cup torn basil leaves

8 eggs

extra basil leaves to garnish

freshly ground black pepper

- Preheat oven to 160°C.
- Lightly spray the capsicums with oil and hold over an open flame or place under a grill, until the skin blisters and blackens. Allow to cool then peel, remove stem and seeds and slice into 1 cm strips.
- Heat a large, ovenproof pan over a medium heat and spray lightly with oil. Cook the onion and garlic gently for a few minutes until soft. Add the spinach leaves and allow to wilt. Add the capsicum, napoli sauce, capers, olives and basil and cook for a few minutes, stirring gently until warmed through.
- Divide mixture between 4 individual ramekins (1½-cup capacity) and crack 2 eggs on top of each. Bake in the oven for 5–7 minutes or until egg whites are cooked but the yolks still soft. Sprinkle torn basil leaves on top, season and serve.

Serves 4

Nutritional Analysis
per Serve

Total kJ: 922

Total calories: 221

Carbohydrates: 11.9 g

Protein: 15.6 g

Fat – total: 11.3 g

Fat – saturated: 3.3 g

Fibre: 4 g

French toast with berries and yoghurt

This favourite breakfast is a great way to use up stale bread. Traditionally, white bread is used but wholemeal or wholegrain are also fine. Also use raspberries when in season.

2 eggs

½ cup no-fat milk

4 slices bread

olive oil spray

2 cups fresh berries (strawberries and blueberries)

½ cup low-fat vanilla yoghurt

- Whisk the eggs and milk together in a shallow dish. Add the bread slices and soak both sides thoroughly in the mixture.
- Heat a large, non-stick frying pan over a medium heat and spray with oil. Cook the bread for 1–2 minutes on each side, or until golden. Serve straight away, topped with berries and a little yoghurt.

Serves 4

Nutritional Analysis
per Serve

Total kJ: 773

Total calories: 184

Carbohydrates: 24 g

Protein: 11 g

Fat – total: 3.9 g

Fat – saturated: 1 g

Fibre: 4.1 g

Baked ricotta with rocket and tomato

Try baby spinach leaves in place of rocket.

olive oil spray

1½ cups low-fat ricotta

2 eggs, lightly beaten

1 cup shredded rocket leaves

2 tablespoons shredded basil leaves,
   plus extra to serve

salt and pepper

4 slices prosciutto

250 g cherry truss tomatoes

Nutritional Analysis
per Serve

Total kJ: 554

Total calories: 132

Carbohydrates: 2.6 g

Protein: 12 g

Fat – total: 8.3 g

Fat – saturated: 4.5 g

Fibre: 0.8 g

- Preheat the oven to 200°C. Grease a 6-hole friand pan with spray oil.
- In a large mixing bowl beat together the ricotta, eggs, rocket and basil until well combined. Season well with salt and pepper. Spoon into the prepared friand pan. Bake for 15–20 minutes, or until the ricotta is set.
- Meanwhile, place the prosciutto slices on an oven tray and bake for 5 minutes. Add the tomatoes to the same tray and bake for a further 5 minutes, or until the prosciutto is crisp and the tomatoes have just started to collapse.
- Invert the baked ricotta onto serving plates and serve with the prosciutto and tomatoes. Top with extra basil leaves.

Serves 6

Banana smoothie

A quick all-in-one breakfast or instant energy lift for any time of day.

1 ripe banana, roughly chopped

1 tablespoon wheatgerm

¼ teaspoon ground cinnamon

3 tablespoons low-fat natural yoghurt

½ teaspoon honey

¾ cup low-fat milk

- Place all ingredients in a blender and mix until smooth. Drink immediately.

Serves 1

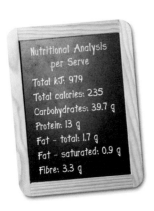

Nutritional Analysis
per Serve

Total kJ: 979
Total calories: 235
Carbohydrates: 39.7 g
Protein: 13 g
Fat - total: 1.7 g
Fat - saturated: 0.9 g
Fibre: 3.3 g

Bacon and asparagus frittata

Delicious hot or cold, this makes a great breakfast to get you started for a busy day. Serve with a grilled tomato and some rocket.

olive oil spray

2 rashers rindless shortcut bacon, chopped

6 eggs

¼ cup grated low-fat cheese

1 bunch chives, snipped

salt and pepper

2 bunches asparagus, ends trimmed, blanched

- Preheat the oven to 180°C.
- Heat a 20 cm non-stick frying pan over a medium heat and spray lightly with oil. Cook the bacon until golden brown, stirring occasionally. Whisk together the eggs, cheese and chives and season well with salt and pepper. Arrange the asparagus spears over the bacon and pour on the egg mixture, being careful not to disturb the asparagus.
- Cook for 4–5 minutes, until the base of the frittata has set. Transfer the pan to the oven and cook for 10–15 minutes, until the frittata is golden and set. Cut into wedges to serve.

VARIATIONS

- Nutritional analysis based on recipe using 2 whole eggs plus 4 egg whites.

Serves 4

Nutritional Analysis
per Serve

Total kJ: 811
Total calories: 193
Carbohydrates: 1.1 g
Protein: 19.7 g
Fat – total: 12 g
Fat – saturated: 4.3 g
Fibre: 0.8 g

Nutritional Analysis
per Serve

Total kJ: 571
Total calories: 136
Carbohydrates: 1 g
Protein: 16.8 g
Fat – total: 7 g
Fat – saturated: 2.7 g
Fibre: 0.8 g

Capsicum, chive and cheese damper

This recipe can be easily adapted to make scones. Simply cut rounds from the dough using a scone cutter and cook as for the damper.

2 cups self-raising flour

¼ teaspoon salt

1 chargrilled capsicum, chopped

½ cup grated low-fat cheese

1 bunch chives, snipped

1 cup buttermilk

Nutritional Analysis
per Serve

Total kJ: 655
Total calories: 156
Carbohydrates: 27 g
Protein: 7.5 g
Fat – total: 1.6 g
Fat – saturated: 0.8 g
Fibre: 1.4 g

- Preheat the oven to 230°C. Line an oven tray with baking paper.
- Sift the flour and salt into a large mixing bowl. Add the capsicum, cheese and chives and mix to combine. Make a well in the centre. Add the buttermilk to the dry ingredients and stir with a flat-bladed knife to form a soft dough.
- Turn the dough out onto a floured surface and shape into a 20 cm round. Lift onto the prepared oven tray and score the top into 8 wedges. Bake for 15–20 minutes until golden brown. The damper should sound hollow when tapped.

Serves 8

Poached egg and creamed spinach on muffins

The secret to perfect poached eggs has a lot to do with freshness. Always check the expiry date on the egg carton and refrigerate after purchase.

olive oil spray

2 bunches English spinach, trimmed and rinsed

1 tablespoon extra-light thickened cream

2 teaspoons Dijon mustard

4 eggs

2 wholemeal English muffins, halved and lightly toasted

pinch of sumac

- Heat a non-stick frying pan over a medium heat and spray with oil. Cook the spinach, stirring, until the leaves have just wilted. Stir in the cream and mustard and simmer over a low heat for 2 minutes.
- Meanwhile, poach the eggs until cooked to your liking. Arrange the toasted muffin halves on 4 serving plates and spoon on the creamed spinach. Top with a poached egg, sprinkle with a little sumac and serve straight away.

Serves 4

Nutritional Analysis per Serve

Total kJ: 769

Total calories: 183

Carbohydrates: 12.2 g

Protein: 14.5 g

Fat – total: 7 g

Fat – saturated: 2.4 g

Fibre: 6.3 g

Herb and cheese egg white omelette

Whisking the egg whites gives this omelette a delightfully light texture. Serve with a grilled tomato or sautéed mushrooms.

4 eggs, separated

3 teaspoons plain flour

salt and pepper

2 tablespoons no-fat milk

2 tablespoons chopped basil leaves

2 tablespoons chopped parsley leaves

2 tablespoons chervil leaves

olive oil spray

¼ cup grated low-fat cheddar cheese

Nutritional Analysis
per Serve

Total kJ: 449
Total calories: 107
Carbohydrates: 2.2 g
Protein: 13.4 g
Fat – total: 9.2 g
Fat – saturated: 2.7 g
Fibre: 0.2 g

- Whisk together 2 of the egg yolks with 1½ teaspoons of the flour and season well with salt and pepper. Add 1 tablespoon of milk and half the herbs.

- Using an electric mixer, whisk 2 of the egg whites until stiff peaks form. Gently fold into the yolk mixture.

- Heat a 20 cm non-stick omelette pan over a medium heat and spray with oil. Pour in the egg mixture and cook until the base is just set. Sprinkle on half the cheese and place the omelette under a preheated grill for 1-2 minutes, or until the omelette has puffed up and the cheese has melted.

- Fold the omelette over and slide onto a serving plate. Use the remaining ingredients to make a second omelette.

Serves 4

Stewed apple and rhubarb

Rhubarb is available all year round but is best in winter when the stalks are thicker and have a more intense colour. Wonderful served on porridge.

2 bunches (1.5 kg) rhubarb, washed, trimmed and de-stringed, then cut into 4 cm lengths

3 apples, peeled, cored and diced

1 cinnamon stick

2 star anise

1 vanilla bean, split lengthwise

½ cup caster sugar

3 tablespoons water

- Place all ingredients in a large saucepan. Cover and cook over a medium heat, stirring occasionally, for 5-7 minutes or until the fruit is tender. Serve hot or refrigerate once cooled.

Serves 4

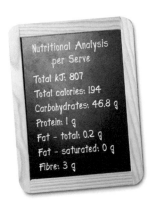

Nutritional Analysis
per Serve

Total kJ: 807

Total calories: 194

Carbohydrates: 46.8 g

Protein: 1 g

Fat - total: 0.2 g

Fat - saturated: 0 g

Fibre: 3 g

Poached fruit with vanilla Frûche

You can use almost any fruit you have on hand for this quick and easy breakfast.

2 cups water

½ cup caster sugar

1 cinnamon stick

2 strips of orange peel

2 peaches, halved

1 orange, segmented

⅓ cup low-fat vanilla Frûche

- Place the water, sugar, cinnamon and orange peel in a medium saucepan. Stir over a low heat until sugar has dissolved. Increase the heat to high and simmer for 10 minutes. Remove from the heat and add the fruit. Stir briefly, then set aside for 10 minutes for the flavours to infuse.
- Serve the fruit drizzled with a little syrup and a dollop of Frûche.

VARIATION

- Nutritional analysis based on recipe replacing sugar with Splenda and Frûche with low-fat vanilla yoghurt.

Serves 4

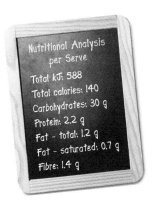

Nutritional Analysis
per Serve

Total kJ: 588
Total calories: 140
Carbohydrates: 30 g
Protein: 2.2 g
Fat – total: 1.2 g
Fat – saturated: 0.7 g
Fibre: 1.4 g

Nutritional Analysis
per Serve

Total kJ: 227
Total calories: 54
Carbohydrates: 10 g
Protein: 2.1 g
Fat – total: 0.1 g
Fat – saturated: 0 g
Fibre: 1.4 g

Ricotta pancakes with bananas and honey

A great weekend favourite that the whole family will enjoy. The batter makes enough for eight pancakes.

250 g low-fat ricotta

2 eggs, lightly beaten

1 cup no-fat milk

1 cup self-raising flour

1 tablespoon caster sugar

1 teaspoon baking powder

olive oil spray

2 bananas, sliced

2 tablespoons honey

- Whisk together the ricotta, eggs and milk. Sift the flour, caster sugar and baking powder into a large mixing bowl. Make a well in the centre and pour in the wet ingredients. Whisk until smooth.
- Heat a non-stick frying pan over a medium heat and spray with oil. Pour ¼ cup of the batter into the pan and cook for 3 minutes until bubbles appear on the surface. Flip over and cook for a further minute, or until golden. Remove from the pan and keep warm while you cook the remaining pancakes.
- Serve the pancakes topped with banana slices and drizzled with a little honey.

VARIATION

- Nutritional analysis based on recipe using no caster sugar, ½ cup low-fat milk, and 2 teaspoons of honey.

Serves 4

Nutritional Analysis
per Serve
Total kJ: 1487
Total calories: 354
Carbohydrates: 53 g
Protein: 15.9 g
Fat - total: 8.5 g
Fat - saturated: 4.4 g
Fibre: 2.4 g

Nutritional Analysis
per Serve
Total kJ: 1310
Total calories: 312
Carbohydrates: 42.3 g
Protein: 15.9 g
Fat - total: 8.5 g
Fat - saturated: 4.4 g
Fibre: 2.4 g

Soups

Vegetable stock

Home-made vegetable stock adds so much flavour to vegetable-based soups and rice dishes. It's suitable for freezing so you can always have some on hand.

3 onions, quartered

½ bunch celery, trimmed and
   cut into 5 cm lengths

2 carrots, peeled and cut into
   5 cm pieces

1 head garlic, cut in half widthwise

5 black peppercorns

2 fresh or dried bay leaves

4 litres water

- Place all ingredients in a large saucepan or stockpot and bring to the boil. Reduce heat and simmer for 1½ hours. Strain the vegetables and reserve liquid in containers ready to freeze once cooled.

Makes 3 litres

Chicken stock

Nothing beats the flavour of home-made stock. Chicken carcasses are available at most butchers.

4 chicken carcasses, washed

5 litres water

2 sticks celery, cut into 5 cm lengths

2 onions, quartered

5 cloves garlic, crushed

10 black peppercorns

3 fresh or dried bay leaves

· Place the carcasses in a large saucepan or stockpot and fill with water until just covered (about 5 litres). Bring to the boil and skim off any scum that rises to the surface. Add the remaining ingredients, reduce heat and gently simmer for 3 hours. Remove from the heat and skim again. Allow to cool then strain into containers and store in the fridge or freezer.

Makes 3 litres

Bacon, lentil and tomato soup

A lovely, hearty soup for winter, and suitable for freezing.

olive oil spray

2 onions, diced

2 cloves garlic, crushed

1 stick celery, diced

4 rashers rindless bacon,
   trimmed and chopped

4 sprigs thyme

½ cup brown lentils, rinsed

1 x 400 g can reduced-salt
   chopped tomatoes

4 cups water

2 fresh or dried bay leaves

4 tablespoons chopped
   coriander leaves

* Note: a 400 g can of lentils may
  be used instead of dried lentils.
  If using canned, reduce the cooking
  time to 20 minutes.

- Heat a large saucepan over a low heat and spray lightly with oil. Add onions, garlic and celery and cook gently for a few minutes until soft. Add bacon and thyme and cook for a further 2 minutes. Add lentils, tomatoes, water and bay leaves, increase heat and bring to the boil. Reduce the heat, cover and simmer for 1 hour, stirring occasionally, until lentils are tender.
- Remove bay leaves and thyme and serve topped with coriander leaves.

Serves 4

Nutritional Analysis
per Serve

Total kJ: 773

Total calories: 186

Carbohydrates: 14.9 g

Protein: 14.8 g

Fat – total: 6.2 g

Fat – saturated: 2.2 g

Fibre: 5.4 g

Minted pea soup

This soup is delicious in summer, topped with harissa for a spicy twist.

olive oil spray

2 onions, finely diced

2 cloves garlic, crushed

3 cups chicken stock (page 61)

500 g frozen peas

1 cup roughly chopped mint leaves

2 tablespoons harissa*

* Harissa paste is available
   from delicatessens.

- Heat a large saucepan over a low heat and spray lightly with oil. Cook the onions and garlic gently for a few minutes until soft. Add chicken stock and bring to the boil. Add peas and bring back to the boil for 5–7 minutes.

- Remove from the heat and allow to cool slightly. Add mint leaves and purée using a blender or hand-held processor. Serve topped with a swirl of harissa if desired. The soup will keep in the fridge for up to 4 days, but is best served immediately as its vibrant green colour will fade.

Serves 4

Nutritional Analysis
per Serve

Total kJ: 504

Total calories: 121

Carbohydrates: 13.8 g

Protein: 9.7 g

Fat – total: 1.2 g

Fat – saturated: 0.3 g

Fibre: 8.1 g

Lamb and barley hotpot

Barley is related to wheat and has a nutty flavour. This is a wonderfully hearty soup for winter.

olive oil spray

1 onion, diced

3 cloves garlic, crushed

2 sticks celery, diced

2 carrots, diced

300 g lamb chuck fillets, trimmed
   and cut into cubes

3 sprigs rosemary

2 tablespoons tomato paste

1½ litres chicken stock (page 61)

2 fresh or dried bay leaves

1 cup pearl barley

125 g green beans, cut into
   4 cm lengths

2 tablespoons chopped
   flat-leaf parsley

- Heat a large saucepan over a low heat and spray lightly with oil. Add onion, garlic, celery and carrots and cook gently for a few minutes until soft. Add lamb and rosemary and cook until the meat is browned on all sides. Cover with napoli sauce and cook for a further 2 minutes. Add the chicken stock and bay leaves and bring to the boil.
- Add the barley and reduce heat. Cover and simmer gently for 1½ hours until the barley is tender. Add beans and simmer for another 30 minutes until tender.
- Remove the bay leaves and rosemary sprigs and serve sprinkled with parsley.

Serves 4

Nutritional Analysis
per Serve

Total kJ: 1085

Total calories: 260

Carbohydrates: 17.1g

Protein: 26 g

Fat – total: 8.2 g

Fat – saturated: 4 g

Fibre: 6.4 g

Spicy dhal soup

Dhal is the name of a spicy Indian dish made from dried lentils that traditionally accompanies curries. Here we have used the same principle but turned it into a delicious soup.

1 cup red split lentils, rinsed

juice of 1 lime

1 teaspoon ground turmeric

1 teaspoon rice bran oil

1 onion, chopped

4 cloves garlic, crushed

1 teaspoon ground cumin

1 teaspoon ground coriander

¼ teaspoon chilli powder

1 x 400 g can reduced-salt
chopped tomatoes

1½ cups water

½ cup coriander leaves, to serve

½ cup low-fat natural yoghurt,
to serve

- Place the rinsed lentils, lime juice and turmeric in a saucepan. Add enough water to cover the lentils by 3 cm. Bring to the boil over a medium heat and cook for 45 minutes, or until lentils are tender.
- Heat the oil in a saucepan over a medium heat. Cook the onion and garlic for 5 minutes, or until the onion is soft. Add the spices and cook for 1 minute, until fragrant. Stir in the tomatoes and ½ cup of water and simmer for 5 minutes. Add the cooked lentils and a further cup of water to the tomato mixture. Simmer for 5 minutes, to warm through.
- When ready to serve, stir in the coriander, ladle into bowls and top with a dollop of yoghurt.

Serves 4

Nutritional Analysis
per Serve

Total kJ: 802
Total calories: 191
Carbohydrates: 24 g
Protein: 14 g
Fat – total: 2.5 g
Fat – saturated: 0.3 g
Fibre: 8.7 g

Beetroot and leek soup

If time is short you can use canned beetroot, but the flavour is much richer and smokier with roasted fresh beets.

2 bunches beetroot, trimmed
and washed
1 head garlic, unpeeled
salt and pepper
1 teaspoon rice bran oil
1 leek, chopped
4 cups water
¼ cup low-fat natural yoghurt,
to serve
snipped chives, to serve

Nutritional Analysis
per Serve
Total kJ: 311
Total calories: 74
Carbohydrates: 10.3 g
Protein: 3 g
Fat – total: 12 g
Fat – saturated: 0.2 g
Fibre: 5 g

- Preheat the oven to 200°C. Place the beetroot and garlic head in an oven tray. Season well with salt and pepper and cover with foil. Bake for 55 minutes, or until the beets are tender. Set aside to cool. Using disposable rubber gloves peel the beetroot and chop them roughly. Squeeze the soft garlic cloves from their skins.

- Heat the oil in a large saucepan over a low heat. Add the leek and cook, covered, for 5 minutes, or until soft. Add the beetroot, garlic and 4 cups of water to the pan. Bring to the boil, then reduce the heat to low and simmer for 15 minutes. Purée with a hand blender and season to taste. Ladle into bowls and serve topped with a dollop of yoghurt and a sprinkling of chives.

Serves 6

Roasted tomato and capsicum soup

For a vegetarian option use vegetable stock (page 60) in place of chicken stock.

800 g roma tomatoes, halved

2 red capsicums

1 teaspoon rice bran oil

1 onion, chopped

1 teaspoon smoked paprika

1 medium potato, chopped

3 cups chicken stock (page 61)

1 tablespoon extra-light sour cream, to serve

Nutritional Analysis
per Serve

Total kJ: 500
Total calories: 119
Carbohydrates: 13.5 g
Protein: 7 g
Fat - total: 3 g
Fat - saturated: 1 g
Fibre: 4 g

- Preheat the oven to 200°C.
- Place the tomatoes and capsicums on an oven tray and bake for 30 minutes, or until the capsicum skins are charred and the tomatoes have collapsed. Place the capsicums in a plastic bag, seal and leave to cool completely. Set the tomatoes aside to cool. Peel and discard the skins from both the tomatoes and capsicums.
- Heat the oil in a large saucepan over a medium heat. Cook the onion for 5 minutes, stirring occasionally, until soft. Add the paprika and stir for 1 minute, until fragrant. Add the roasted tomatoes and capsicums to the pan with the potato and stock and bring to the boil. Reduce the heat to low and simmer for 30 minutes.
- Purée with a hand blender and strain into a clean saucepan. Reheat gently over a low heat. Ladle into bowls and serve topped with a dollop of sour cream.

Serves 4

Corn chowder

Use a 400 g can of sweet corn in place of the fresh corn cobs, if you prefer.

1 teaspoon rice bran oil

1 leek, halved and chopped

2 cloves garlic, crushed

1 tablespoon flour

4 cups chicken stock (page 61)

3 corn cobs, kernels removed
with a knife

1 x 310 g can creamed corn

1 zucchini, diced

salt and pepper

chopped parsley leaves

- Heat the oil in a saucepan over a medium heat. Cook the leek and garlic for 5 minutes, or until the leek is soft but not brown. Add the flour and stir over a low heat for 2 minutes. Pour in the stock and whisk to combine. Increase the heat to high and simmer for 5 minutes, stirring occasionally.
- Add the corn kernels, creamed corn and zucchini to the pan. Simmer for 10 minutes then remove from the heat. Season well with salt and pepper. Just before serving, stir in the parsley.

Serves 4

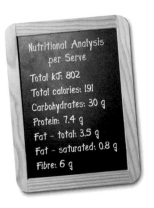

Nutritional Analysis
per Serve

Total kJ: 802
Total calories: 191
Carbohydrates: 30 g
Protein: 7.4 g
Fat – total: 3.5 g
Fat – saturated: 0.8 g
Fibre: 6 g

Mushroom and lentil broth

Swiss brown mushrooms have a stronger, earthier flavour than button mushrooms and help to give this soup richness and depth.

1 cup green lentils, rinsed

2 sticks celery, chopped

1 onion, chopped

1 x 400 g can reduced-salt
    chopped tomatoes

1/3 cup tomato paste

1 teaspoon rice bran oil

250 g button mushrooms, sliced

250 g Swiss brown mushrooms, sliced

chopped parsley leaves, to serve

Nutritional Analysis
per Serve

Total kJ: 949

Total calories: 226

Carbohydrates: 27 g

Protein: 17.7g

Fat – total: 2.7 g

Fat – saturated: 0.3 g

Fibre: 14 g

- Place the rinsed lentils in a large saucepan, cover with water and bring to the boil over a high heat. Drain and return the lentils to the pan. Cover with 6 cups of water and bring to a simmer over a medium heat. Add the celery, onion, tomatoes and tomato paste and simmer for 40 minutes.

- Meanwhile, heat the oil in a frying pan over a high heat. Cook the mushrooms for 5 minutes, or until golden. Add to the soup and simmer for 20 minutes, or until the lentils are completely tender and the soup has slightly thickened.

- Ladle into serving bowls and serve topped with chopped parsley.

Serves 4

Seafood, fennel and saffron chowder

This soup is a meal in itself. Serve it with crusty bread to soak up the juices.

1 teaspoon olive oil

1 onion, chopped

1 small fennel bulb, thinly sliced,
 tips reserved

2 cloves garlic, crushed

pinch of saffron threads

dash of Tabasco sauce

2 x 400 g cans reduced-salt
 chopped tomatoes

1 cup water

8 green (raw) prawns, peeled
 and deveined, tails intact

8 mussels, scrubbed and
 beards removed

200 g firm white fish, cubed

200 g salmon, cubed

pepper

· Heat the oil in a large saucepan over a
 medium heat. Cook the onion, fennel and
 garlic for 5 minutes, or until soft but not
 coloured. Add the saffron and Tabasco
 and stir to combine. Add the tomatoes and
 water and bring to the boil. Reduce the
 heat to low and simmer for 15 minutes,
 or until the soup has thickened slightly.

· Add the prawns, mussels, fish and salmon
 to the pan and simmer for 3–5 minutes,
 or until the prawns and fish are cooked
 and the mussels have opened. Discard
 any mussels that do not open. Season well
 with pepper. Ladle into serving bowls and
 just before serving top with the reserved
 fennel tips.

Serves 4

Nutritional Analysis
per Serve

Total kJ: 1134
Total calories: 270
Carbohydrates: 11.2 g
Protein: 37 g
Fat – total: 7.6 g
Fat – saturated: 1.6 g
Fibre: 3.3 g

Salads

Roasted vegetable and couscous salad

This salad is a satisfying meal. The vegetables can be pre-roasted and combined with the other ingredients when ready to serve.

¼ butternut pumpkin, peeled, seeded
   and cut into 2 cm pieces
olive oil spray
½ eggplant, cut into 2 cm cubes
1 zucchini, cut into 2 cm pieces
¾ cup couscous
¾ cup boiling water
½ red onion, finely sliced
½ red capsicum, finely sliced
150 g baby rocket leaves

DRESSING
1 clove garlic, crushed
2 teaspoons red wine vinegar
1 teaspoon balsamic vinegar
⅓ cup extra-virgin olive oil
¼ teaspoon honey

- Preheat oven to 250ºC.
- Place pumpkin pieces in a deep baking tray and spray lightly with oil to coat. Bake for 10 minutes then add the eggplant and zucchini (also sprayed lightly with oil). Roast for a further 20 minutes or until cooked. Remove from oven and set aside.
- Combine the couscous and boiling water in a bowl, mix with a fork, cover with plastic wrap and let stand for 7 minutes.
- To make the dressing place all ingredients in an airtight jar and shake until combined.
- Loosen the couscous with a fork until light and fluffy. Add the roast vegetables, onion, capsicum and rocket leaves. Mix the dressing through the salad until coated.

Serves 4

Nutritional Analysis
per Serve

Total kJ: 801
Total calories: 192
Carbohydrates: 11.7 g
Protein: 4.2 g
Fat – total: 13 g
Fat – saturated: 1.5 g
Fibre: 5.6 g

Chicken, beetroot and walnut salad

A sweet and colourful summer salad with a nutty crunch.

4 large beetroot, washed and trimmed

2 medium skinless chicken breasts

150 g baby spinach leaves

2 tablespoons roughly chopped walnuts

½ red onion, thinly sliced

DRESSING

1 clove garlic, crushed

2 teaspoons red wine vinegar

1 teaspoon balsamic vinegar

⅓ cup extra-virgin olive oil

¼ teaspoon honey

- Preheat oven to 150°C.
- Wrap each beetroot in foil and roast on an oven rack for 1½-2 hours until soft. Allow to cool then peel and slice into 8 wedges.
- Grill or chargrill the chicken breasts for 5 minutes on each side until cooked through. Allow to cool slightly and cut into 2½ cm slices.
- To make the dressing place all ingredients in an airtight jar and shake to combine.
- Combine the spinach leaves, walnuts and onion in a bowl then add the chicken and beetroot. Toss the dressing through the salad and serve warm.

Serves 4

Nutritional Analysis
per Serve

Total kJ: 1336

Total calories: 321

Carbohydrates: 5.5 g

Protein: 35.1 g

Fat – total: 16.9 g

Fat – saturated: 3.9 g

Fibre: 3 g

Tabbouleh

This salad is a wonderful accompaniment for lamb cutlets. It can be made in advance and the dressing added when ready to serve.

2 tablespoons coarse burghul (bulgar wheat)
2 tablespoons boiling water
1½ cups (roughly 1 bunch) finely chopped flat-leaf parsley
¼ cup finely chopped mint leaves
1 tomato, seeds removed, diced
1 red onion, finely diced
1 teaspoon ground cinnamon
½ teaspoon ground allspice

DRESSING
juice of 2 lemons
1 clove garlic, crushed
½ cup extra-virgin olive oil
¼ cup flaxseed oil

- Place burghul and water in a bowl and set aside for 10 minutes.
- To make the dressing place all ingredients in an airtight jar and shake until combined.
- Combine parsley, mint, tomato and onion in a mixing bowl. Loosen the burghul with your fingertips to separate the grains. Add to the other ingredients along with the cinnamon and allspice. Toss the dressing through and serve.

Serves 4

Nutritional Analysis
per Serve

Total kJ: 642
Total calories: 154
Carbohydrates: 6.4 g
Protein: 2 g
Fat – total: 12.5 g
Fat – saturated: 1.5 g
Fibre: 2.8 g

Fennel and orange salad

Fennel has a lovely aniseed flavour and is a good palate cleanser. This salad goes well with fish, chicken or pork dishes.

2 medium fennel bulbs, trimmed and
   finely sliced lengthwise
2 oranges, peeled and cut into segments
½ red onion, finely sliced
¼ cup flat-leaf parsley
1 radicchio lettuce, shredded

DRESSING
juice of 2 lemons
1 clove garlic, crushed
½ cup extra-virgin olive oil
¼ cup flaxseed oil

- Place the fennel in a bowl of iced water for 5 minutes (this will make it crisper and sweeter).
- To make the dressing place all ingredients in an airtight jar and shake until combined.
- Drain the fennel and combine all salad ingredients. Toss the dressing through until well coated.

Nutritional Analysis
per Serve
Total kJ: 706
Total calories: 169
Carbohydrates: 9.7 g
Protein: 2.1 g
Fat – total: 12.5 g
Fat – saturated: 1.5 g
Fibre: 4.9 g

Tuna and asparagus salad

You can assemble this salad so quickly – it's perfect to take to work.

1 x 425 g can tuna in springwater

2 bunches asparagus, sliced into
  7 cm lengths

½ cup corn kernels

½ red capsicum, finely sliced

4 spring onions, finely sliced

50 g mixed lettuce leaves

½ cup coriander leaves

DRESSING

1 tablespoon Dijon mustard

1½ teaspoons seeded mustard

1 tablespoon low-fat natural yoghurt

1½ teaspoons white wine vinegar

juice of 1 lemon

• Drain the tuna. Steam the asparagus
for 3–5 minutes until tender then allow
to cool. To make the dressing place
all ingredients in an airtight jar and
shake until combined. Combine all salad
ingredients and drizzle with dressing.

Serves 4

Nutritional Analysis
per Serve

Total kJ: 825

Total calories: 198

Carbohydrates: 9.6 g

Protein: 30 g

Fat – total: 3.2 g

Fat – saturated: 1.1 g

Fibre: 3.7 g

Chargrilled asparagus, bocconcini and watercress salad

Bocconcini translates to 'little mouthfuls' and they are simply baby balls of mozzarella. The vegetables for this salad may be cooked on a barbecue or griddle, or roasted in a moderate oven.

olive oil spray

4 slices Italian-style crusty bread

2 bunches asparagus, ends trimmed

1 bunch watercress, leaves picked

6 baby bocconcini, halved

2 tablespoons chopped capers

2 tablespoons balsamic vinegar

- Preheat the oven to 180°C. Lightly spray 2 oven trays with oil. Arrange the bread in a single layer on one baking tray and arrange the asparagus on the other. Spray each with a little more oil and bake for 10 minutes, or until the bread is golden and crisp and the asparagus is tender.
- Place a slice of toasted bread on each plate. Top each with some asparagus spears, watercress, bocconcini and capers. Drizzle with balsamic vinegar just before serving.

VARIATION

- Nutritional analysis based on recipe using 2 small pieces of Italian bread.

Serves 4

Nutritional Analysis
per Serve

Total kJ: 882
Total calories: 210
Carbohydrates: 10.8 g
Protein: 14.6 g
Fat – total: 11.4 g
Fat – saturated: 6.5 g
Fibre: 2 g

Nutritional Analysis
per Serve

Total kJ: 727
Total calories: 173
Carbohydrates: 4 g
Protein: 13.3 g
Fat – total: 11 g
Fat – saturated: 6.5 g
Fibre: 1.6 g

Chickpea, fennel and onion salad

Dried chickpeas can be used in place of canned. Soak them overnight, then drain and simmer in a pan of boiling water for 45 minutes, or until tender.

1 x 220 g can chickpeas, rinsed
and drained

1 small fennel bulb, thinly sliced

1 small red onion, halved and
thinly sliced

250 g cherry tomatoes, halved

½ cup chopped parsley leaves

2 tablespoons lemon juice

1 teaspoon honey

1 teaspoon wholegrain mustard

- In a large mixing bowl, toss together the chickpeas, fennel, onion, tomatoes and parsley.
- In a separate bowl, whisk together the lemon juice, honey and mustard.
- Drizzle the dressing over the salad and toss gently to combine.

Serves 4

Nutritional Analysis
per Serve

Total kJ: 353
Total calories: 84
Carbohydrates: 11 g
Protein: 4 g
Fat – total: 1.3 g
Fat – saturated: 0.2 g
Fibre: 4 g

Lite caesar salad

An all-time favourite meal that can still be enjoyed when following a healthy eating plan.

2 slices wholemeal bread, crusts removed, cut into cubes
2 rashers rindless shortcut bacon, chopped
2 anchovies, drained and halved (optional)
1 baby cos lettuce, leaves separated
1 tablespoon grated parmesan cheese

DRESSING
¼ cup low-fat natural yoghurt
2 tablespoons lemon juice
1 tablespoon Dijon mustard
1 teaspoon Worcestershire sauce
1 clove garlic, crushed
dash of Tabasco sauce

- Preheat the oven to 180°C. Line 2 oven trays with baking paper. Place the bread cubes on one baking tray and the bacon on the other. Bake for 15 minutes, or until the bread is golden and crisp and the bacon is cooked. Set aside to cool.
- To make the dressing, whisk all the ingredients together until well combined.
- Pat the anchovies with kitchen paper to remove any excess oil. Place in a large mixing bowl with the bread cubes, bacon, lettuce and parmesan. Drizzle on the dressing and toss to combine.

Serves 4

Nutritional Analysis
Salad

Total kJ: 344
Total calories: 82
Carbohydrates: 6 g
Protein: 7 g
Fat – total: 3 g
Fat – saturated: 1.1 g
Fibre: 1 g

Nutritional Analysis
Dressing

Total kJ: 59
Total calories: 14
Carbohydrates: 1.5 g
Protein: 1 g
Fat – total: 0.2 g
Fat – saturated: 0 g
Fibre: 0.3 g

Snow pea sprout and herb salad

Lamb's lettuce (also known as mâche) is very popular in France and is now being grown here. The delicious dark green leaves are perfect in this light salad. Use baby spinach leaves or rocket if unavailable.

100 g snow pea sprouts

1 cup mint leaves

1 cup coriander leaves

1 cup torn basil leaves

100 g lamb's lettuce (mâche)

2 Lebanese cucumbers, halved, seeded and thinly sliced

1 small red onion, finely chopped

DRESSING

2 tablespoons lime juice

2 teaspoons fish sauce

½ teaspoon brown sugar

- Combine all the salad ingredients in a large mixing bowl.
- Whisk together the dressing ingredients and drizzle over the salad. Toss to combine and serve straight away.

Serves 4

Nutritional Analysis
Dressing

Total kJ: 21
Total calories: 5
Carbohydrates: 0.7 g
Protein: 0.3 g
Fat – total: 0 g
Fat – saturated: 0 g
Fibre: 0 g

Nutritional Analysis
Salad

Total kJ: 273
Total calories: 65
Carbohydrates: 10 g
Protein: 3.8 g
Fat – total: 0 g
Fat – saturated: 0 g
Fibre: 3.6 g

Artichoke, tat soi and prosciutto salad

Tat soi, sometimes called bok choy rosette, is a leafy, dark green salad vegetable that grows in a perfect flat rosette. If you can't find tat soi, then baby spinach leaves make a good substitute.

4 slices prosciutto

1 large tat soi rosette or 100 g loose
   tat soi leaves

2 x 400 g cans artichoke hearts, drained

200 g baby grape tomatoes, halved

½ cup basil leaves

2 spring onions, trimmed and chopped

2 tablespoons lemon juice

1 teaspoon extra-virgin olive oil

1 teaspoon Dijon mustard

- Preheat the oven to 180°C. Lay the prosciutto rashers on an oven tray and bake for 10 minutes, or until crisp. Set aside to cool.
- Break the tat soi leaves from the rosette and wash thoroughly. Pat dry then place in a salad bowl with the artichokes, tomatoes, basil and spring onion. Whisk together the lemon juice, oil and mustard and pour over the salad. Break up the prosciutto with your hands and add to the salad. Toss well to combine and serve straight away.

Serves 4

Nutritional Analysis
per Serve

Total kJ: 399
Total calories: 95
Carbohydrates: 4 g
Protein: 8.7 g
Fat - total: 3.1 g
Fat - saturated: 0.6 g
Fibre: 7 g

Moroccan-style carrot and sumac salad

Sumac is a dark red berry that has been dried and then crushed. It has a sharp fruity flavour and is commonly used in Middle Eastern cooking. If sumac is unavailable then you could use paprika instead.

5 medium carrots, peeled and cut into matchsticks

3 cloves garlic, peeled

2 tablespoons lemon juice

¼ cup chopped parsley leaves

¼ cup chopped coriander leaves

1 teaspoon sumac

1 teaspoon flaked almonds

- Place the carrots and garlic in a large saucepan and cover with water. Bring to the boil over a medium heat and cook for 10 minutes, or until the carrots are tender. Drain, discard the garlic and tip the carrots into a mixing bowl. Stir in the lemon juice and leave to cool.
- When cool, add the parsley and coriander and toss to combine. Sprinkle with sumac and almonds before serving.

Serves 6

Nutritional Analysis
per Serve

Total kJ: 105
Total calories: 25
Carbohydrates: 3 g
Protein: 0.7 g
Fat – total: 0.3 g
Fat – saturated: 0 g
Fibre: 2 g

Potato, pea and mint salad

This salad is always a favourite. Making the dressing with yoghurt is a great way to reduce the energy content.

400 g baby potatoes
2 cups frozen peas, blanched
1 small red onion, finely chopped
¼ cup low-fat natural yoghurt
¼ cup shredded mint leaves
1 teaspoon lemon juice
½ teaspoon horseradish

- Cook the potatoes in a pan of boiling water for 15 minutes, or until tender. Drain and cut the potatoes in half. Place in a large mixing bowl with the peas and onion.
- Mix together the yoghurt, mint, lemon juice and horseradish. Add to the salad and toss gently to combine.

Serves 4

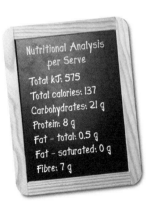

Nutritional Analysis
per Serve
Total kJ: 575
Total calories: 137
Carbohydrates: 21 g
Protein: 8 g
Fat - total: 0.5 g
Fat - saturated: 0 g
Fibre: 7 g

Moroccan beetroot and coriander salad

Beetroot will stain your hands, so use disposable plastic gloves when peeling.

1 bunch beetroot, ends trimmed

½ cup chopped coriander leaves

½ cup torn mint leaves

½ cup low-fat natural yoghurt

1 tablespoon lemon juice

1 teaspoon finely grated lemon zest

1 teaspoon sumac

Nutritional Analysis
per Serve

Total kJ: 315

Total calories: 75

Carbohydrates: 11.3 g

Protein: 4 g

Fat – total: 0.2 g

Fat – saturated: 0 g

Fibre: 4 g

- Place the beetroot in a large saucepan of boiling water and cook for 40 minutes, or until tender. Drain and set aside to cool completely. Peel the beetroot and chop it roughly. Place in a salad bowl with the mint and coriander.
- Whisk together the yoghurt and lemon juice. Tip into a small serving bowl and top with the lemon zest and sumac. Serve the beetroot salad with the dressing on the side.

Serves 4

Tomato and mozzarella salad

Buffalo mozzarella is made from buffalo milk and has half the fat content of cow's milk mozzarella.

250 g grape tomatoes, halved

250 g yellow grape tomatoes, halved

100 g buffalo mozzarella, roughly torn

100 g lamb's lettuce (mâche) or
   snow pea sprouts

2 tablespoons white wine vinegar

1 teaspoon olive oil

salt and pepper

- Combine the tomatoes, mozzarella and lettuce in a salad bowl.
- Whisk together the vinegar and oil and season well with salt and pepper. Drizzle over the salad and toss to combine.

Serves 6

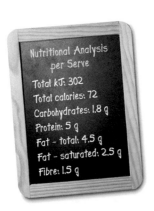

Nutritional Analysis
per Serve

Total kJ: 302
Total calories: 72
Carbohydrates: 1.8 g
Protein: 5 g
Fat – total: 4.5 g
Fat – saturated: 2.5 g
Fibre: 1.5 g

Bulgur wheat pilaf

Bulgur wheat is also known as burghul and is most commonly used in the salad tabbouleh. This recipe makes a heartier dish that can be served as a warm or room temperature salad. Alternatively, serve it on its own as a light meal or as an accompaniment to Tandoori Chicken Skewers (page 182), Spice-crusted Lamb Fillet (page 198) or Chermoula-crusted Beef (page 214).

1 teaspoon rice bran oil

1 onion, chopped

1 tablespoon Cajun seasoning mix

1 cup fine bulgur wheat

3 cups chicken stock (page 61)

salt and pepper

½ cup sultanas

½ cup chopped coriander leaves

1 tablespoon flaked toasted almonds

Nutritional Analysis
per Serve

Total kJ: 706
Total calories: 168
Carbohydrates: 45 g
Protein: 8 g
Fat – total: 4 g
Fat – saturated: 0.7 g
Fibre: 8.7 g

- Heat the oil in a non-stick frying pan over a medium heat. Cook the onion for 5 minutes, or until soft. Add the Cajun seasoning mix and stir for 30 seconds, until fragrant. Stir in the bulgur wheat and cook for 3 minutes, stirring constantly. Add the stock and bring to the boil. Reduce the heat to low, cover the pan and simmer for 20 minutes, or until all the stock has been absorbed.
- Season well with salt and pepper and stir in the sultanas. Cover the pan and set aside for 10 minutes. Fluff up the pilaf with a fork and top with the coriander and flaked almonds. Serve warm or at room temperature.

Serves 4

Cucumber, mango and mint salad

Choose unblemished, sweet-smelling mangoes. Cut the cheeks from the mango and thinly slice the flesh. Scoop any remaining flesh away from the skin and stone with a large spoon.

3/4 cup mint leaves

1/4 cup lime juice

1 teaspoon olive oil

1 teaspoon brown sugar

2 Lebanese cucumbers, quartered lengthways

2 mangoes, thinly sliced

finely grated zest of 1 lime

- Place 1/2 cup of the mint leaves in a small blender or food processor with the lime juice, oil and brown sugar. Process until smooth.
- Place the cucumbers, mango slices and remaining mint leaves in a salad bowl. Drizzle on the dressing and toss gently to combine. Serve topped with lime zest.

Serves 4

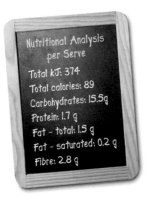

Nutritional Analysis
per Serve

Total kJ: 374
Total calories: 89
Carbohydrates: 15.5g
Protein: 1.7 g
Fat – total: 1.5 g
Fat – saturated: 0.2 g
Fibre: 2.8 g

Lemongrass, prawn and noodle salad

This is a wonderfully refreshing weekend salad. The beansprouts and peanuts give this dish a delicious crunch.

2 stalks lemongrass, white part only, finely chopped

1 long red chilli, seeded and finely chopped

4 kaffir lime leaves, finely shredded

2 teaspoons grated ginger

¼ cup lime juice

1 teaspoon fish sauce

16 green (raw) prawns, peeled and deveined, tails intact

SALAD

150 g bean thread noodles

2 cups trimmed beansprouts

1 cup coriander leaves

1 cup torn mint leaves

¼ cup lime juice

2 tablespoons fish sauce

2 tablespoons sweet chilli sauce

½ teaspoon sugar

2 tablespoons chopped unsalted roasted peanuts

- Combine the lemongrass, chilli, kaffir lime leaves, ginger, lime juice and fish sauce in a bowl. Add the prawns and turn them to coat well in the marinade. Cover and refrigerate for 2 hours.
- Place the noodles in a bowl and cover with boiling water. Leave to soak for 5 minutes until soft, then drain well and place in a large mixing bowl. Add the beansprouts and fresh herbs. In a separate bowl, whisk together the lime juice, fish sauce, sweet chilli sauce and sugar. Add to the noodles and toss to combine.
- Cook the prawns on a preheated chargrill or barbecue for 2 minutes on each side, or until pink and firm.
- Divide the noodle salad between serving plates and top with the prawns and a sprinkling of peanuts.

Serves 4

Nutritional Analysis per Serve

Total kJ: 773

Total calories: 184

Carbohydrates: 15 g

Protein: 20 g

Fat – total: 3.5 g

Fat – saturated: 0.4 g

Fibre: 4 g

Smoked salmon niçoise

Traditionally a niçoise salad has tuna as an ingredient, but why not try smoked salmon as a delicious change to this classic?

100 g green beans, chopped, and
    blanched

100 g baby spinach leaves

4 cocktail potatoes, boiled and quartered

2 Lebanese cucumbers, halved, seeded
    and sliced

1 small red onion, halved and thinly sliced

100 g smoked salmon, sliced

DRESSING

¼ cup lemon juice

1 teaspoon olive oil

1 clove garlic, crushed

1 teaspoon Dijon mustard

- Place the beans, spinach, potato, cucumbers and onion in a large mixing bowl.
- Whisk together the dressing ingredients and pour over the salad. Toss to combine.
- Divide the salad among serving plates and top with slices of smoked salmon.

Serves 6

Nutritional Analysis
Dressing

Total kJ: 42
Total calories: 10
Carbohydrates: 0.4 g
Protein: 0.1 g
Fat – total: 0.8 g
Fat – saturated: 0.1 g
Fibre: 0.1 g

Nutritional Analysis
Salad

Total kJ: 286
Total calories: 68
Carbohydrates: 7.6 g
Protein: 6 g
Fat – total: 0.9 g
Fat – saturated: 0.2 g
Fibre: 2.3 g

Asian-style coleslaw

A delicious twist on traditional coleslaw. For an interesting presentation, try serving all the ingredients stacked in a wombok leaf.

¼ wombok (Chinese cabbage), shredded

1 carrot, grated

1 cup trimmed beansprouts

3 spring onions, trimmed and chopped

1 red capsicum, finely sliced

1 cup coriander leaves

½ teaspoon chilli flakes

¼ cup chopped unsalted roasted
   peanuts

DRESSING

½ cup lime juice

1 tablespoon fish sauce

1 teaspoon grated ginger

1 teaspoon sugar

- Place all the salad ingredients, except the peanuts, in a large mixing bowl and toss to combine.
- To make the dressing, mix all the ingredients together to combine.
- Toss the dressing through the salad, top with chopped peanuts and serve straight away.

Serves 4

Nutritional Analysis
Dressing

Total kJ: 21
Total calories: 5
Carbohydrates: 1 g
Protein: 0.2 g
Fat – total: 0 g
Fat – saturated: 0 g
Fibre: 0 g

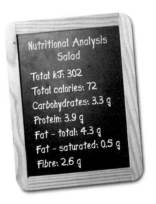

Nutritional Analysis
Salad

Total kJ: 302
Total calories: 72
Carbohydrates: 3.3 g
Protein: 3.9 g
Fat – total: 4.3 g
Fat – saturated: 0.5 g
Fibre: 2.6 g

Calamari and asparagus salad

If calamari tubes are unavailable, use calamari rings instead.

2 calamari tubes, cleaned

2 cloves garlic, crushed

1 long red chilli, finely chopped

1 teaspoon grated ginger

¼ cup lemon juice

2 bunches asparagus, ends trimmed

100 g baby rocket leaves

Nutritional Analysis
per Serve

Total kJ: 281
Total calories: 67
Carbohydrates: 2 g
Protein: 11.4 g
Fat - total: 1 g
Fat - saturated: 0.2 g
Fibre: 1.4 g

- Split the calamari tubes along one side and open out flat. Slice thinly lengthways into strips.
- Place the garlic, chilli, ginger and lemon juice in a mixing bowl.
- Preheat a chargrill or barbecue on high. Cook the calamari for 2 minutes until opaque. Remove from the grill and add to the garlicky marinade. Toss to coat and set aside.
- Cook the asparagus on the chargrill for 2 minutes, or until tender.
- To serve, mound the rocket and asparagus on a serving platter. Scatter on the calamari, together with the marinade, and toss gently to combine. Serve straight away.

Serves 4

Coconut chicken salad

Poaching chicken is a great way to infuse flavour and to keep the meat tender and moist.

1 x 375 ml can Light & Creamy Coconut Flavoured Evaporated Milk
1 tablespoon grated ginger
1 teaspoon fish sauce
400 g skinless chicken breast fillets
salt and pepper
2 Lebanese cucumbers, halved lengthways, seeded and sliced
2 sticks celery, chopped
1 cup coriander leaves
¼ teaspoon chilli flakes

- Heat the evaporated milk, ginger and fish sauce in a saucepan over a medium heat, until just simmering. Reduce the heat to low, add the chicken breasts and simmer gently for 15 minutes. Remove the pan from the heat and stand for 10 minutes.
- Remove the chicken from the stock and shred finely. Place the shredded chicken in a salad bowl. Strain the coconut stock and return 1 cup to a small saucepan. Bring to the boil over a high heat and boil for 5 minutes, or until reduced by half. Season well with salt and pepper and allow to cool slightly before pouring over the shredded chicken.
- Add the cucumber, celery and coriander to the bowl and toss to combine. Sprinkle with chilli flakes and serve.

Serves 4

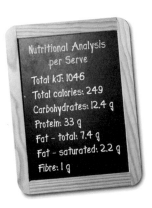

Nutritional Analysis per Serve

Total kJ: 1046
Total calories: 249
Carbohydrates: 12.4 g
Protein: 33 g
Fat – total: 7.4 g
Fat – saturated: 2.2 g
Fibre: 1 g

Ginger pork and papaya salad

Rice wine vinegar is available from Asian grocers and some supermarkets. Substitute white wine vinegar if you prefer.

400 g pork fillet, thinly sliced

1 tablespoon soy sauce

1 tablespoon finely grated ginger

2 cloves garlic, crushed

olive oil spray

100 g snow peas, blanched and halved

2 bunches rocket, trimmed and rinsed

1 small papaya, peeled and chopped

2 tablespoons sweet chilli sauce

1 tablespoon rice wine vinegar

- Combine the pork slices, soy sauce, ginger and garlic in a bowl. Cover and refrigerate for 30 minutes.
- Heat a non-stick frying pan over a high heat and spray with oil. Cook the pork in batches for 2–3 minutes, or until browned and cooked through.
- Place the pork in a salad bowl with the snow peas, rocket and papaya. Mix together the chilli sauce and vinegar, drizzle over the salad and toss to combine.

Serves 4

Nutritional Analysis
per Serve

Total kJ: 655

Total calories: 156

Carbohydrates: 6 g

Protein: 24 g

Fat – total: 3 g

Fat – saturated: 0.9 g

Fibre: 2.4 g

Snacks and light meals

Chickpea, fetta and coriander tarts

These savoury tarts are easy to make and are great for picnics.

1 x 400 g can chickpeas, rinsed and
   drained
1 cup tomato passata
100 g reduced-fat fetta, crumbled
½ cup chopped coriander leaves
freshly ground black pepper
1 egg
4 sheets filo pastry
olive oil spray

Nutritional Analysis
per Serve
Total kJ: 995
Total calories: 239
Carbohydrates: 23 g
Protein: 16.6 g
Fat – total: 7.6 g
Fat – saturated: 3.1 g
Fibre: 6.1 g

- Preheat oven to 220°C.
- Place the chickpeas in a mixing bowl and mash with a fork. Add the passata, fetta and coriander and mix together well. Season with pepper to taste then stir in egg.
- Lay a sheet of filo on the bench, keeping the remainder covered to prevent them from drying out. Spray the sheet lightly with oil and fold in half. Repeat this once then cut in half, giving you 2 rectangles of pastry.
- Spray a muffin tin lightly with oil and line each mould with a filo piece, pressing it down around the base and edges. Fill the moulds evenly with the chickpea mixture and bake for 20 minutes or until the pastry is golden brown.

Makes 8 tarts (2 per serve)

Corn fritters with smoked salmon and coriander dressing

A light and satisfying meal, perfect for weekend lunches.

DRESSING

1 cup chopped coriander leaves

juice of ½ lemon

2 cloves garlic, roughly chopped

2 small red chillies, seeded and
    finely sliced

5 tablespoons low-fat natural yoghurt

½ cup wholemeal self-raising flour

¼ teaspoon baking powder

2 spring onions, finely sliced

1 tablespoon chopped dill

1 x 200 g cooked corn cob, kernels
    removed, or 200 g can corn kernels

4 tablespoons low-fat milk

2 egg whites

olive oil spray

freshly ground black pepper

8 slices smoked salmon, cut into 5 cm
    pieces

125 g watercress

¼ red onion, finely sliced

- To make the dressing place coriander, lemon juice, garlic and chillies in a food processor and process to a smooth paste. Add the yoghurt and set aside.
- Combine flour, baking powder, spring onions, dill and corn in a mixing bowl. Add milk and stir thoroughly.
- In another bowl whisk egg whites until fluffy then gently fold through the flour mixture.
- Heat a large frying pan over a medium heat and spray lightly with oil. Spoon the mixture into the pan and cook until small bubbles form on the surface.
- Turn the fritters over and cook for a further 5 minutes or until golden.
- Combine the salmon, watercress and onion and arrange on top of the fritters. Drizzle with coriander dressing. The dressing will keep for up to 3 days stored in an airtight container in the fridge.

Serves 4

Nutritional Analysis
per Serve

Total kJ: 1095
Total calories: 263
Carbohydrates: 29 g
Protein: 21 g
Fat – total: 5 g
Fat – saturated: 1.1 g
Fibre: 5.6 g

Stuffed jacket potatoes

Here are a few ways to turn baked potatoes into a satisfying light meal.

4 medium potatoes

- Preheat the oven to 180°C. Wrap each potato in aluminium foil and bake for about 1 hour, or until tender. Scoop the centre from each potato and chop roughly. Add to the filling of your choice and use to fill the potatoes.

Serves 4

COLESLAW FILLING

1 cup shredded cabbage
1 carrot, grated
1 spring onion, trimmed and chopped
¼ cup low-fat mayonnaise
⅓ cup grated low-fat cheese

- Combine all ingredients except for the cheese in a bowl. Add chopped potato (see above) and mix well. Sprinkle a little cheese into each hot potato and top with coleslaw.

TUNA, LEMON AND CAPER FILLING

1 x 425 g can tuna in springwater, drained and flaked
1 tablespoon low-fat mayonnaise
2 teaspoons sweet chilli sauce
1 teaspoon lemon juice
1 teaspoon finely grated lemon zest
1 teaspoon baby capers
1 small red chilli, finely chopped

- Combine all ingredients in a bowl. Add chopped potato (see above) and mix well. Fill potatoes while still warm.

See also
Chilli con Carne
(page 130).

Nutritional Analysis
per Serve
Total kJ: 433
Total calories: 103
Carbohydrates: 20 g
Protein: 3.6 g
Fat – total: 0.2 g
Fat – saturated: 0 g
Fibre: 3 g

Nutritional Analysis
per Serve
Total kJ: 433
Total calories: 103
Carbohydrates: 7 g
Protein: 5.2 g
Fat – total: 7 g
Fat – saturated: 3 g
Fibre: 2 g

Zucchini and cottage cheese open sandwich

There are many different vegetables to use for this sandwich instead of zucchini. Top with chopped gherkin, tomato, capsicum or even pumpkin for a delicious change.

2 zucchini, ends trimmed

olive oil spray

200 g low-fat cottage cheese

2 tablespoons snipped chives

1 tablespoon sweet chilli sauce

1 teaspoon mustard

4 slices sourdough bread, toasted

- Use a vegetable peeler to slice the zucchini lengthways into ribbons.
- Heat a chargrill on high. Spray the zucchini ribbons with oil and cook for 2 minutes, or until tender.
- Combine the cottage cheese, chives, sweet chilli sauce and mustard in a mixing bowl. Divide between the toast slices and serve topped with zucchini ribbons.

Serves 4

Nutritional Analysis
per Serve

Total kJ: 433
Total calories: 103
Carbohydrates: 10.6 g
Protein: 11 g
Fat – total: 1.3 g
Fat – saturated: 0.5 g
Fibre: 2 g

Roasted mushrooms
with ricotta and rocket

Use your choice of field, cup or button mushrooms for this dish.

4 large flat mushrooms

2 roma tomatoes, halved

1 zucchini, halved lengthways

2 cloves garlic, peeled

olive oil spray

1 tablespoon balsamic vinegar

¼ cup fresh wholegrain breadcrumbs

1 tablespoon thyme leaves

salt and pepper

50 g low-fat ricotta, crumbled

1 bunch rocket

· Preheat the oven to 180°C.
· Place the mushrooms, tomatoes, zucchini and garlic in an oven tray. Spray with oil and sprinkle on the balsamic vinegar. Mix together the breadcrumbs and thyme and scatter over the vegetables. Season well with salt and pepper and crumble on the ricotta. Bake for 30 minutes, or until the vegetables are tender and the topping golden.
· Serve with rocket leaves.

Serves 4

Nutritional Analysis
per Serve

Total kJ: 214
Total calories: 51
Carbohydrates: 5 g
Protein: 4 g
Fat – total: 1.6 g
Fat – saturated: 0.7 g
Fibre: 2.3 g

Chilli con carne wraps

Chilli con carne is a great favourite and endlessly versatile. As well as serving it with steamed rice for a filling meal, try using it as a stuffing for jacket potatoes – or serve it on toast for breakfast. It's a terrific dish to have on hand in the freezer.

1 teaspoon olive oil

1 onion, chopped

200 g premium lean beef mince

1 x 400 g can reduced-salt chopped tomatoes

2 tablespoons reduced-salt tomato paste

1 cup diced Queensland blue pumpkin

¼ cup water

1 x 420 g can kidney beans, rinsed and drained

1 teaspoon chilli sauce

salt and pepper

lettuce leaves

4 pieces lavash or mountain bread

- Heat the oil in a large saucepan over a medium heat. Cook the onion for 5 minutes, or until tender. Increase the heat to high, add the mince to the pan and cook for 5 minutes, or until brown. Stir well to break up any lumps. Stir in the tomatoes, tomato paste, pumpkin and ¼ cup of water. Simmer for 15 minutes, or until the pumpkin is tender and the mince is cooked. Add the kidney beans and chilli sauce and season to taste with salt and pepper. Simmer for 5 minutes. Set aside to cool slightly.

- Arrange a few lettuce leaves on top of each piece of lavash. Top with the chilli con carne and roll up to form a wrap. If taking the wraps for lunch or a picnic, seal well in plastic wrap.

Makes 4

Nutritional Analysis
per Serve

Total kJ: 1285
Total calories: 306
Carbohydrates: 35 g
Protein: 22 g
Fat – total: 6 g
Fat – saturated: 2 g
Fibre: 11 g

Potato, rocket and ricotta pizza

Pizza doesn't have to be a high-calorie treat. With just a few changes you can fit it into any healthy-eating plan.

4 small pita breads

¾ cup low-fat ricotta

2 cloves garlic, crushed

salt and pepper

3 medium potatoes, boiled and sliced

1 cup grated low-fat mozzarella cheese

1 bunch rocket leaves

¼ teaspoon chilli flakes

- Preheat the grill to high. Line an oven tray with baking paper. Place the pita breads on the prepared tray and cook under the grill on one side only for 1 minute, or until crisp and golden.
- Combine the ricotta and garlic and season well with salt and pepper. Spread over the un-toasted side of the pita and top with potato slices. Sprinkle with mozzarella and cook under the grill for 3–5 minutes, or until the cheese has melted and is beginning to colour. Scatter on the rocket leaves and chilli flakes and serve straight away.

Serves 4

Nutritional Analysis
per Serve

Total kJ: 1445

Total calories: 344

Carbohydrates: 38.5 g

Protein: 21 g

Fat – total: 10.7 g

Fat – saturated: 6.3 g

Fibre: 3.3 g

Spinach and ricotta gnocchi

A delicious, light way to eat gnocchi.

1 teaspoon olive oil

1 onion, finely chopped

2 cloves garlic, crushed

2 x 400 g cans reduced-salt chopped
tomatoes

½ cup basil leaves

½ cup water

salt and pepper

GNOCCHI

½ bunch English spinach, trimmed
and rinsed

200 g low-fat ricotta

1 egg, lightly beaten

½ cup plain flour

salt and pepper

1 tablespoon grated parmesan cheese,
to serve

- To make the gnocchi, finely shred the spinach leaves and place in a large mixing bowl with the ricotta. Mix until combined. Add the egg and flour and mix well. Season to taste with salt and pepper. Roll teaspoons of the mixture into balls and flatten slightly with the back of a fork. Lay the gnocchi on a clean tray, cover and refrigerate for 30 minutes.
- Meanwhile, heat the oil in a large frying pan over a medium heat. Cook the onion and garlic for 5 minutes, or until the onion is tender. Add the tomatoes, basil and ½ cup of water and simmer for 5 minutes, or until the sauce has thickened slightly. Season to taste with salt and pepper.
- Bring a large saucepan of water to the boil. Reduce the heat to low and cook the gnocchi in batches for 1 minute, or until they rise to the top. Drain well. Divide the tomato sauce between 4 serving bowls and add the gnocchi. Sprinkle with a little parmesan and serve straight away.

Serves 4

Nutritional Analysis
per Serve

Total kJ: 966

Total calories: 230

Carbohydrates: 22.2 g

Protein: 13.5 g

Fat – total: 8.3 g

Fat – saturated: 3.7 g

Fibre: 6 g

Penne with silverbeet, chilli and capers

This quick and easy pasta meal is full of flavour.

300 g penne

1 teaspoon olive oil

1 bunch silverbeet, trimmed, washed and shredded

2 rashers rindless shortcut bacon, chopped

2 cloves garlic, sliced

2 small red chillies, finely chopped

finely grated zest of 1 lemon

2 tablespoons lemon juice

2 teaspoons capers

- Cook the penne in a large saucepan of boiling water according to the packet instructions. Drain and keep warm.
- Heat the oil in a large frying pan over a medium heat. Cook the silverbeet, stirring regularly, for 5 minutes, or until wilted. Add the bacon and cook for a further 5 minutes. Stir in the remaining ingredients and cook for 2 minutes.
- Add the penne to the pan and stir for 2 minutes, until warmed through.

Serves 4

Nutritional Analysis
per Serve

Total kJ: 1310

Total calories: 312

Carbohydrates: 53 g

Protein: 13.5 g

Fat - total: 4 g

Fat - saturated: 1 g

Fibre: 4 g

Mushroom wontons in ginger broth

Shitake mushrooms have a stronger flavour than button mushrooms and make an ideal filling for dumplings. If shitake mushrooms are unavailable then Swiss brown mushrooms can be used instead.

100 g shitake mushrooms, finely chopped

¼ cup water chestnuts

2 cloves garlic, crushed

1 lime leaf, finely chopped

2 tablespoons oyster sauce

2 teaspoons fish sauce

12 round gow gee wrappers

BROTH

4 cups chicken stock (page 61)

1 cup water

2 tablespoons soy sauce

2 cm piece of ginger, peeled and
   shredded

4 spring onions, trimmed and cut
   into thirds

1 bunch bok choy, leaves separated

- Combine the mushrooms, water chestnuts, garlic, lime leaf, oyster sauce and fish sauce in a bowl. Heat a small frying pan over a medium heat. Cook the mushroom mixture for 3 minutes until soft. Set aside to cool.
- Place a teaspoon of the cool mushroom mixture in the centre of each wrapper. Wet the edges with a little water and fold over to form a half circle, pressing the edges together to seal.
- Heat the chicken stock, water, soy sauce and ginger in a large saucepan over a medium heat. Simmer for 5 minutes. Reduce the heat to low and add the spring onions and dumplings. Simmer gently for 3-5 minutes, or until the dumplings have risen to the surface.
- Divide the bok choy leaves between 4 serving bowls and ladle on the ginger broth and dumplings.

Serves 4

Nutritional Analysis
per Serve

Total kJ: 592

Total calories: 141

Carbohydrates: 22 g

Protein: 7.2 g

Fat – total: 2 g

Fat – saturated: 0.7 g

Fibre: 2.7 g

Steamed salmon with ginger paste

Salmon is loaded with omega-3 fatty acids, which makes this a healthy light meal.

3 cloves garlic, crushed

1 tablespoon grated ginger

1 tablespoon lime juice

1 tablespoon fish sauce

1 teaspoon sugar

1 Lebanese cucumber

4 x 80 g salmon fillets, skin removed

1 cup steamed rice, to serve

- Place the garlic, ginger, lime juice, fish sauce and sugar in a small bowl and mix together well. Use a vegetable peeler to slice the cucumber into ribbons and add to the paste. Toss to combine.
- Place each salmon fillet on a piece of baking paper. Divide the cucumber mixture between the salmon pieces, spreading evenly to coat. Wrap the salmon up in the baking paper to form a parcel.
- Line a metal or bamboo steamer with baking paper and sit over a wok or saucepan of simmering water. Steam the fish parcels, covered, for 5–8 minutes.
- Carefully unwrap the salmon parcels and serve with steamed rice.

Serves 4

Nutritional Analysis
per Serve

Total kJ: 827

Total calories: 197

Carbohydrates: 16.6 g

Protein: 18 g

Fat – total: 6.1 g

Fat – saturated: 1.3 g

Fibre: 1.2 g

Cannellini bean and avocado nachos

Nachos are always a firm family favourite, and with this recipe you can enjoy them without the high calorie count.

1 piece Lebanese bread, cut into wedges

olive oil spray

1 teaspoon olive oil

2 cloves garlic, crushed

1 small red chilli, chopped

1 teaspoon ground coriander

1 teaspoon ground cumin

1 x 400 g can cannellini beans, rinsed and drained

1 x 400 g can reduced-salt chopped tomatoes

1/2 avocado, chopped

1/4 cup coriander leaves

1 tablespoon low-fat sour cream, to serve

- Preheat the oven to 180°C. Place the Lebanese bread on a baking tray and spray with oil. Bake for 8-10 minutes, or until golden and crisp.
- Heat the oil in a saucepan over a medium heat. Cook the garlic and chilli for 1 minute. Add the spices and cook for a further minute, until fragrant. Stir in the beans and tomatoes and simmer for 8-10 minutes.
- Arrange the toasted bread pieces on a serving platter. Top with the bean mixture and scatter on the avocado and coriander. Serve with a dollop of sour cream.

Serves 4

Nutritional Analysis
per Serve

Total kJ: 1197
Total calories: 285
Carbohydrates: 32 g
Protein: 12.5 g
Fat – total: 10.2 g
Fat – saturated: 2.5 g
Fibre: 9.7 g

Crab tartlets

The tart shells can be made ahead of time and stored in an airtight container. Fill just before serving so the pastry stays crisp.

olive oil spray

4 sheets filo pastry

1 x 170 g can crab meat

2 tablespoons chopped coriander

1½ tablespoons 99% fat-free mayonnaise

1 tablespoon sweet chilli sauce

1 tablespoon lime juice

Nutritional Analysis
per Serve

Total kJ: 122
Total calories: 29
Carbohydrates: 3.5 g
Protein: 2.3 g
Fat – total: 0.6 g
Fat – saturated: 0 g
Fibre: 0.2 g

- Preheat the oven to 200°C.
- Spray a 12-hole mini muffin pan with oil.
- Spray each sheet of filo pastry with oil and stack them on top of each other on a clean work surface. Using a 7 cm round cutter, cut 12 circles from the pastry and use to line the holes of the muffin pan. Bake for 5 minutes, until golden and crisp. Carefully remove the pastry shells from the pan and leave to cool.
- In a mixing bowl, combine the crab meat, coriander, mayonnaise, sweet chilli sauce and lime juice and mix well. Just before serving fill the pastry cases with the crab mix.

Makes 12

Prawn and pork san choy bau

There are many versions of san choy bau, although it is perhaps most commonly made with minced beef. We have given another option here by using plump fresh prawns with pork mince. They make a great combination.

1 iceberg lettuce

1 teaspoon rice bran oil

200 g pork mince

2 cloves garlic, crushed

2 teaspoons grated ginger

1 small red chilli, finely chopped

10 green (raw) prawns, peeled, deveined and chopped

2 tablespoons water

1 tablespoon reduced-salt soy sauce

1 teaspoon sugar

4 spring onions, trimmed and chopped

½ cup coriander leaves

finely grated zest and juice of 1 lime

- Separate whole leaves from the lettuce. Wash them well, then pat dry and refrigerate until needed.
- Heat the oil in a wok or large frying pan over a high heat. Cook the pork mince, garlic, ginger and chilli for 5 minutes until brown. Add the prawns and stir-fry for 3 minutes, or until pink and firm.
- In a small bowl, mix together the water, soy sauce and sugar. Add to the pan and simmer for 1 minute. Stir in the spring onion, coriander, lime juice and zest and toss to combine.
- Spoon the prawn and pork mixture into lettuce cups and serve straight away.

Serves 4

Nutritional Analysis
per Serve

Total kJ: 344
Total calories: 82
Carbohydrates: 2.4 g
Protein: 12 g
Fat – total: 1.7 g
Fat – saturated: 0.2 g
Fibre: 2.8 g

Tuna and cucumber sushi

The thought of rolling sushi can often scare people away from making their own. These sushi squares avoid the rolling issue – they are as simple as making a sandwich.

1½ cups sushi rice

2 cups water

2 tablespoons rice vinegar

1 teaspoon sugar

4 sheets nori (seaweed)

1 x 425 g can tuna in springwater, drained and flaked

2 tablespoons low-fat mayonnaise

3 Lebanese cucumbers, cut into thin sticks

reduced-salt soy sauce, to serve

wasabi, to serve

- Place the rice and water in a large saucepan. Cover and bring to the boil over a high heat. Reduce the heat to very low and cook, covered, for 15 minutes. Remove from the heat and leave to stand for 10 minutes. Do not remove the lid.
- Mix together the vinegar and sugar and stir through the rice. Spread the rice out on a shallow tray. Set aside to cool completely.
- Lay a nori sheet on a flat surface. Spread a quarter of the rice evenly on the nori. Mix together the tuna and mayonnaise. Spread half of the flaked tuna mix over the rice and top with half of the cucumber sticks. Spread on another quarter of the rice and top with a sheet of nori. Use a sharp knife to cut into 6 rectangles. Repeat with the remaining ingredients to make a total of 12 pieces.
- Serve with soy sauce and wasabi for dipping.

Makes 12

Nutritional Analysis
per Serve

Total kJ: 626
Total calories: 149
Carbohydrates: 22 g
Protein: 11 g
Fat – total: 1.6 g
Fat – saturated: 0.5 g
Fibre: 0.8 g

Steamed pork dumplings

Asian dumplings are a delicious snack; once tried you will be hooked. Look out for a double-height bamboo steamer at Asian supermarkets. You'll find it invaluable for cooking all sorts of healthy steamed dishes.

400 g lean pork mince
2 spring onions, trimmed and chopped
¼ cup chopped coriander leaves
2 tablespoons oyster sauce
2 tablespoons reduced-salt soy sauce
2 teaspoons grated ginger
1 small red chilli, finely chopped
1 clove garlic, crushed
30 round gow gee wrappers

DIPPING SAUCE
⅓ cup reduced-salt soy sauce
2 teaspoons sugar
1 teaspoon white vinegar
1 clove garlic, sliced
2 drops sesame oil

- Place all the ingredients, except for the wrappers, in a bowl and mix well to combine. Place a teaspoon of the mixture in the centre of each wrapper. Wet the edges with a little water and pleat them together to seal.
- Line a metal or bamboo steamer with baking paper and sit over a wok or saucepan of simmering water. Steam the dumplings in batches, covered, for 10–15 minutes. Transfer the cooked dumplings to a warm bowl and leave covered with aluminium foil while you cook the rest.
- Meanwhile, combine the dipping sauce ingredients in a small bowl. Serve the steamed dumplings with the dipping sauce.

Makes 30

Nutritional Analysis
per Dumpling
Total kJ: 172
Total calories: 41
Carbohydrates: 4 g
Protein: 3.5 g
Fat – total: 1 g
Fat – saturated: 0.4 g
Fibre: 0.2 g

Nutritional Analysis
of Dipping Sauce
Total kJ: 17
Total calories: 4
Carbohydrates: 0.4 g
Protein: 0.4 g
Fat – total: 0 g
Fat – saturated: 0 g
Fibre: 0 g

Spicy beef and mushroom kebabs

These are fantastic done on the barbecue. Use any combination of vegetables.

MARINADE

2 tablespoons grated ginger

2 cloves garlic, crushed

juice of 2 limes

2 small red chillies, seeded and
    finely sliced

½ cup oyster sauce

1 teaspoon sesame oil

2 tablespoons vegetable oil

500 g lean beef, cut into cubes

2 corn cobs, husks removed and cut into
    2½ cm rounds

1 red capsicum, cored, seeded and cut
    into squares

1 zucchini, cut into 2½ cm rounds

1 red onion, cut into wedges

8 flat mushrooms, wiped, stalks
    removed, and cut in half

- Combine marinade ingredients and pour over beef pieces, tossing to coat. Marinate overnight or for a minimum of 2 hours.
- If using bamboo skewers, soak in water for 30 minutes.
- Steam corn for 5-7 minutes or until tender.
- Thread alternating pieces of beef and vegetables onto skewers. Use any leftover marinade to baste during cooking.
- Place skewers under a hot grill and cook for for 8-10 minutes, turning once. Serve with a salad of mixed green leaves.

Serves 4

Nutritional Analysis
per Serve

Total kJ: 1230

Total calories: 295

Carbohydrates: 11.4 g

Protein: 37 g

Fat - total: 10.2 g

Fat - saturated: 4.3 g

Fibre: 3.3 g

Lamb and pine nut pizza

This pizza base is easy to make and is enough for a 12-inch pizza. Alternatively you could use a piece of pita bread.

BASE
2½ cups wholemeal self-raising flour
3 heaped tablespoons low-fat natural yoghurt

olive oil spray
250 g lamb fillets, trimmed
3 tablespoons tomato paste
½ red onion, finely sliced
1 tablespoon pine nuts
50 g baby rocket leaves
2 tablespoons low-fat natural yoghurt

- Preheat oven to 220°C.
- Sift the flour into a mixing bowl, make a well in the centre and add the yoghurt. Mix well to form a smooth dough. Press dough into a lightly greased pizza tray so that it covers the base evenly (about 1 cm thick).
- Heat a large frying pan over a medium heat and spray lightly with oil. Add the lamb and brown on all sides. Transfer to an ovenproof dish and cook for a further 5 minutes in the oven. Remove, allow to cool slightly and cut into 1 cm slices. Keep warm.
- Bake pizza base for 7 minutes until golden around the edges. Remove base from oven, top with napoli sauce and arrange onion and lamb slices. Bake for a further 10 minutes.
- Toast the pine nuts in a dry pan over a low heat until golden.
- Serve pizza topped with rocket leaves, pine nuts and yoghurt.

Serves 4

Nutritional Analysis
per Serve
Total kJ: 1884
Total calories: 452
Carbohydrates: 61 g
Protein: 25 g
Fat – total: 8.2 g
Fat – saturated: 1.3 g
Fibre: 11.3 g

Dinners

Vegetables stuffed with spiced rice

These can be served as either a vegetarian main meal or in smaller portions as an entrée or side dish.

2 small eggplants, cut in half lengthwise and skin pierced a couple of times with a skewer

2 zucchini, cut in half lengthwise

2 red capsicums, cut in half lengthwise, cored and seeded

2 tomatoes, cut in half widthwise, seeds removed and saved

STUFFING

olive oil spray

2 onions, finely diced

4 cloves garlic, crushed

3 cups cooked brown rice

1 x 400 g can reduced-salt crushed tomatoes

$1/4$ cup finely shredded mint leaves

juice of 1 lemon

freshly ground black pepper

$1^1/2$ teaspoons cinnamon

$1/2$ teaspoon allspice

- Preheat oven to 200°C.
- Steam eggplants, zucchini and capsicums for 8-10 minutes until tender. Allow to cool, then using a teaspoon gently scrape out the insides (leaving a 1-1$1/2$ cm wall) of the eggplant, zucchini and tomato. Dice the flesh and set aside.
- Heat a large frying pan over a medium heat, spray lightly with oil and cook the onion and garlic gently until soft. Add the eggplant, zucchini and tomato flesh and cook for a further 3 minutes. Add the cooked rice, tomatoes, mint, lemon juice, pepper, cinnamon and allspice.
- Pack the vegetable shells snugly into a baking dish and stuff. Cover the dish with foil and transfer to the oven for 40 minutes. Remove the foil and cook for a further 10 minutes.

Serves 4

Nutritional Analysis
per Serve
Total kJ: 593
Total calories: 142
Carbohydrates: 17.8 g
Protein: 7.8 g
Fat – total: 1.4 g
Fat – saturated: 0.1 g
Fibre: 11.4 g

Pumpkin, ricotta and sage cannelloni

You can omit the white sauce in this recipe for an even healthier dish. You'll need to cook the lasagna sheets in a large pot of boiling water before filling with the pumpkin mixture and baking.

750 g butternut pumpkin, peeled
  and chopped
6 cloves garlic, unpeeled
1 tablespoon torn sage leaves
olive oil spray
salt and pepper
4 sheets fresh lasagna, halved
  widthways
½ cup low-fat ricotta
½ bunch English spinach, trimmed
  and rinsed
2 teaspoons grated parmesan cheese

- Preheat the oven to 200°C. Place the pumpkin, garlic and sage in an oven tray and spray with oil. Season well with salt and pepper and bake for 30 minutes, or until the pumpkin is tender.
- Spray a shallow ovenproof dish with oil. Lay the lasagna sheets on a flat surface and spread lightly with ricotta. Cover with a single layer of spinach and a little of the baked pumpkin. Roll up to form cylinders and place, seam side down, in the prepared dish. Sprinkle with parmesan cheese.
- Cover with foil and bake for 20 minutes. Remove the foil and bake for a further 10 minutes, or until the cannelloni are golden.

Serves 4

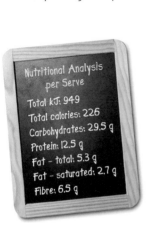

Nutritional Analysis
per Serve
Total kJ: 949
Total calories: 226
Carbohydrates: 29.5 g
Protein: 12.5 g
Fat – total: 5.3 g
Fat – saturated: 2.7 g
Fibre: 6.5 g

Spicy chickpeas with tomato

Chickpeas have a sweet, nutty flavour and are used in many Indian and Mediterranean dishes. Use dried chickpeas in place of canned if you prefer. You'll need to soak them overnight before simmering them in water for 45 minutes, or until tender.

1 teaspoon olive oil

1 onion, chopped

1 teaspoon ground cumin

1 teaspoon ground coriander

1 teaspoon ground turmeric

1 small red chilli, finely chopped

1 x 400 g can chickpeas, rinsed
   and drained

250 g grape tomatoes, halved

¼ cup chopped coriander leaves

crusty bread, to serve

- Heat the oil in a saucepan over a medium heat. Cook the onion for 5 minutes, or until tender. Add the spices and chilli and cook for 1 minute, until fragrant. Add the chickpeas and cook over a low heat for 10 minutes. Stir in the tomatoes and coriander and simmer for 3 minutes.
- Serve with crusty bread.

VARIATION

- Nutritional analysis based on recipe omitting the crusty bread.

Serves 4

Nutritional Analysis
per Serve

Total kJ: 1021
Total calories: 243
Carbohydrates: 36.4 g
Protein: 10.4 g
Fat – total: 4.8 g
Fat – saturated: 0.6 g
Fibre: 7.5 g

Nutritional Analysis
per Serve

Total kJ: 563
Total calories: 134
Carbohydrates: 16.5 g
Protein: 7 g
Fat – total: 3.3 g
Fat – saturated: 0.5 g
Fibre: 6 g

Harissa-spiced vegetable tagine

Harissa is a fiery paste from North Africa. It is made largely from crushed dried chillies, garlic and spices and is very hot! Substitute chilli powder to taste, if you prefer.

olive oil spray

1 onion, chopped

2 cloves garlic, crushed

1 teaspoon harissa paste

1 teaspoon ground cumin

2 potatoes, peeled and chopped

2 carrots, chopped

2 medium kumara (or sweet potato), chopped

3 cups chicken stock (page 61)

finely grated zest of 1 lemon

2 tablespoons lemon juice

1 cup cauliflower florets

1 cup frozen peas

salt and pepper

¼ cup coriander leaves

- Preheat the oven to 180°C.
- Heat a flameproof casserole dish over a medium heat and spray with oil. Cook the onion for 5 minutes, or until tender. Add the garlic, harissa and cumin and cook for 1 minute, until fragrant. Add the potatoes, carrots, kumara and stock. Bring to the boil and stir in the lemon zest and juice. Cover the casserole dish, transfer to the oven and bake for 45 minutes. Stir in the cauliflower and peas and bake, uncovered, for another 10 minutes.
- Season to taste with salt and pepper and stir in the coriander leaves just before serving.

Serves 6

Nutritional Analysis
per Serve

Total kJ: 479

Total calories: 114

Carbohydrates: 17.9 g

Protein: 5.8 g

Fat – total: 0.9 g

Fat – saturated: 0.3 g

Fibre: 4.8 g

Spiced bean loaf

This is a great high-fibre alternative to meatloaf. Serve with a green salad.

olive oil spray

1 onion, finely diced

2 cloves garlic, crushed

2 sticks celery, finely diced

1 x 400 g can lentils, rinsed and drained

1 x 420 g can red kidney beans, rinsed
   and drained

½ zucchini, grated

½ carrot, grated

2 eggs

½ cup tomato passata

1½ tablespoons pine nuts

½ teaspoon ground cumin

½ teaspoon cayenne pepper

1 teaspoon sweet paprika

¾ cup wheatgerm

- Preheat oven to 200°C.
- Line a loaf tin (5-cup capacity) with greaseproof paper. Heat a large frying pan over a medium heat, spray lightly with oil and cook the onion, garlic and celery until soft. Remove from heat and allow to cool.
- Combine the lentils and beans and purée two-thirds of the mix. Stir through remaining beans, onion mixture and the remaining ingredients. Tip into the loaf tin and press firmly into shape.
- Bake in the oven for 50 minutes until the centre of the loaf is firm to the touch. Serve hot or cold.

Serves 4

Nutritional Analysis
per Serve

Total kJ: 1361
Total calories: 327
Carbohydrates: 30.4 g
Protein: 20.3 g
Fat – total: 10.3 g
Fat – saturated: 1.5 g
Fibre: 14 g

Prawns with avocado and mango salsa

A dish that's perfect when entertaining in summer.

600 g green (raw) peeled prawns

1 ripe avocado, cut into 2 cm pieces

1 small red chilli, seeded and finely diced

1 large mango, peeled and diced

   (or 1 x 425 g can mango cheeks,

   drained and diced)

½ red onion, finely diced

juice of 2 limes

¼ cup chopped coriander leaves

¼ cup reduced-fat mayonnaise

- Bring a saucepan of water to the boil, add the prawns and cook for 5 minutes until pink. Drain and allow to cool.
- Mix the avocado, chilli, mango, onion, lime juice and coriander leaves together. Add the mayonnaise and stir until all the ingredients are coated. To serve, spread the salsa on a plate and top with prawns.

Serves 4

Nutritional Analysis
per Serve
Total kJ: 1389
Total calories: 333
Carbohydrates: 12.3 g
Protein: 40.1 g
Fat – total: 12.6 g
Fat – saturated: 2.7 g
Fibre: 2.4 g

Ocean trout panzanella salad

This salad is perfect for entertaining: not only is it extremely colourful and attractive on the plate, it is also very easy to make.

4 x 300 g ocean trout fillets

1½ pieces mountain bread, cut into 5 cm squares

1 red capsicum

olive oil spray

1 tomato, diced

3 tablespoons roughly chopped pitted olives

1 Lebanese cucumber, halved lengthwise, seeded and roughly chopped

½ red onion, finely sliced

2 tablespoons roughly chopped capers

3 tablespoons torn basil leaves

2 tablespoons chopped flat-leaf parsley

4 tablespoons red wine vinegar

4 tablespoons extra-virgin olive oil

- Preheat oven to 150°C.
- Place ocean trout fillets on a lined baking tray and roast in the oven for 10 minutes. When cooked the flesh should separate but remain firm when pressed lightly.
- Arrange the mountain bread squares on a baking tray and place in the oven for about 20 minutes to crispen.
- Spray the capsicum lightly with oil and hold over a flame or under a grill until the skin blackens. Allow to cool, then peel, seed and cut into 2 cm strips.
- Combine the bread, capsicum, tomato, olives, cucumber, onion and capers. Using your fingers, gently flake the ocean trout into the salad. Add the basil and parsley leaves, drizzle vinegar and oil over and mix thoroughly.

Serves 4

Nutritional Analysis
per Serve

Total kJ: 1310
Total calories: 314
Carbohydrates: 7.4 g
Protein: 19.8 g
Fat – total: 22 g
Fat – saturated: 3.5 g
Fibre: 1.3 g

Sardines provençale

This recipe uses canned sardines, but for an interesting variation cook fresh sardines separately first. Sardine bones are soft and edible, and a great source of calcium.

olive oil spray

2 onions, diced

4 cloves garlic, crushed

2 tomatoes, diced

¼ cup white wine

2 tablespoons chopped oregano leaves

1 cup chicken stock (page 61)

400 g canned sardines in springwater, drained

2 tablespoons roughly chopped black olives

2 tablespoons basil leaves

freshly ground black pepper

- Heat a large frying pan over a medium heat and spray lightly with oil. Cook the onions and garlic gently until soft. Add the tomatoes and white wine and cook until the wine has reduced by half. Add the oregano and chicken stock, increase heat and bring to the boil. Cook until the sauce begins to thicken. Add the sardines to the pan and allow to warm through. Add the olives, basil leaves and pepper to taste, and serve immediately.

Serves 4

Nutritional Analysis
per Serve

Total kJ: 907
Total calories: 218
Carbohydrates: 9 g
Protein: 21 g
Fat – total: 9.8 g
Fat – saturated: 2.5 g
Fibre: 2.3 g

Crisp-skinned salmon
with lemon and Asian greens

This dish is simple and tasty. The salt causes the salmon skin to crispen, and also adds wonderful flavour, so use the best-quality salt you can find.

4 x 180–200 g Atlantic salmon fillets,
    skin on
rind (julienned) and juice of 1 lemon
1 teaspoon sea salt flakes
olive oil spray
2 bunches baby bok choy, outer leaves
    removed, and cut into strips

Nutritional Analysis
per Serve

Total kJ: 1245
Total calories: 299
Carbohydrates: 1.1 g
Protein: 37.2 g
Fat – total: 15.7 g
Fat – saturated: 3.7 g
Fibre: 1 g

- Pat the salmon skin dry using a paper towel. Drizzle about a tablespoon of the lemon juice over the skin then coat evenly with salt flakes.
- Heat a large frying pan over a medium-high heat and spray lightly with oil. Cook the salmon skin-side down in the hot pan for 3–5 minutes, gently shaking the pan occasionally to ensure the skin doesn't stick, then carefully flip over and cook for another 3–5 minutes. The salmon should be golden brown and crisp.
- Meanwhile, steam the bok choy for 5 minutes then mix through the lemon rind and remaining lemon juice. Serve salmon fillets with bok choy.

Serves 4

Snapper with Greek salad

Snapper is a firm white fish with a mild flavour. It is very low in fat and high in protein.

olive oil spray

4 x 180–200 g snapper fillets, skin on

SALAD

2 tomatoes, diced

1 Lebanese cucumber, sliced lengthwise,
   seeded and diced

1 red onion, finely sliced

½ teaspoon dried oregano

4 tablespoons roughly chopped
   black olives

4 tablespoons roughly chopped
   flat-leaf parsley

2 tablespoons reduced-fat fetta,
   crumbled

DRESSING

1 clove garlic, crushed

2 teaspoons red wine vinegar

1 teaspoon balsamic vinegar

⅓ cup extra-virgin olive oil

½ teaspoon honey

- Heat a large frying pan over a high heat and spray lightly with oil. Cook the snapper fillets skin-side down for 3–5 minutes, then carefully flip over and cook for 3–5 minutes on the other side, gently moving the pan occasionally to ensure the skin doesn't stick to the pan.
- Combine the tomatoes, cucumber, onion, oregano, olives and parsley in a mixing bowl.
- To make the dressing place all ingredients in an airtight jar and shake until combined. Add the fetta to the salad. Mix the dressing through the salad and serve with snapper fillets on top.

Serves 4

Nutritional Analysis
per Serve

Total kJ: 1436
Total calories: 345
Carbohydrates: 5.8 g
Protein: 51.5 g
Fat – total: 12 g
Fat – saturated: 3.2 g
Fibre: 2 g

Swordfish with roast tomato and rocket salad

A very simple dish with a lovely herb flavour.

3 tomatoes, cut in half widthwise

olive oil spray

1 teaspoon chopped oregano leaves

4 x 180 g swordfish steaks

120 g rocket leaves

¼ cup balsamic vinegar

Nutritional Analysis
per Serve

Total kJ: 1043

Total calories: 250

Carbohydrates: 2.4 g

Protein: 45.8 g

Fat – total: 5.3 g

Fat – saturated: 1.6 g

Fibre: 1.6 g

- Preheat oven to 150°C.
- Place tomatoes on a baking tray, spray lightly with oil and sprinkle with oregano leaves. Roast in the oven for 1 hour until soft.
- Heat a large frying pan over a medium-high heat and spray lightly with oil. Cook the swordfish for 5 minutes on each side until cooked through. Remove from the pan and set aside in a warm place.
- Spray the frying pan again lightly with oil and heat. Chop the tomato halves and place in the heated frying pan. Cook for 1–2 minutes over a high heat then add the rocket. Toss through the tomatoes and allow to wilt slightly. Add the balsamic vinegar and mix through. Remove from the pan and serve immediately with the swordfish.

Serves 4

Fish and chips with tartare sauce

Partially cooking the potatoes in the microwave before baking speeds up the cooking time. It also helps to release the starch from the potatoes, resulting in a crisp, golden crust.

4 medium desirée potatoes, peeled
   and cut into thick chips
olive oil spray
salt and pepper
finely grated zest and juice of 1 lemon
2 tablespoons chopped parsley leaves
4 fillets flathead, snapper or bream
   (about 500 g in total)
Tartare Sauce (page 255), to serve
lemon wedges, to serve

- Preheat the oven to 200°C. Line an oven tray with baking paper.
- Place the potato chips in a microwave-safe plastic bag and microwave on high for 5 minutes. Place the chips on the prepared oven tray and spray with oil. Season with salt and bake for 30 minutes, or until crisp and golden.
- In a shallow dish combine the lemon juice and zest and chopped parsley.
- Season the fish with salt and pepper. Heat a non-stick frying pan over a high heat. Spray with oil and cook the fish for 2 minutes on each side, or until opaque. Remove the fish from the pan and transfer to the dish with the lemon mixture. Turn the fish in the mixture so it is evenly coated.
- Serve the fish and chips with a dollop of tartare sauce and lemon wedges.

Serves 4

Nutritional Analysis
per Serve

Total kJ: 865
Total calories: 206
Carbohydrates: 16.6 g
Protein: 29.5 g
Fat – total: 1.4 g
Fat – saturated: 0.5 g
Fibre: 2.2 g

Fish and leek pie

Leeks are part of the onion family. Trim off the green tops and the roots and just use the pale green and white part. As they are grown under the soil, leeks need to be thoroughly washed before using to remove any lingering dirt.

olive oil spray

2 leeks, chopped

2 teaspoons finely grated lemon zest

1 tablespoon cornflour

2 cups no-fat milk

1 cup water

300 g firm white fish fillets, cubed

200 g salmon fillet, cubed

¼ cup snipped dill

2 boiled potatoes

- Heat a saucepan over a low heat and spray with oil. Cook the leeks and lemon zest for 5 minutes, covered, until the leeks are tender.
- In a small bowl, combine the cornflour and ¼ cup of the milk to form a paste. Add the remaining milk and water to the leeks and bring to the boil. Add the cornflour paste and stir over a medium heat for 3 minutes, until the sauce has thickened. Stir in the fish cubes and the dill and remove from the heat. Spoon into a 4-cup heatproof dish.
- Cut the potatoes into 2 cm slices and arrange over the fish. Spray with oil and cook under a hot grill for 5 minutes, until the potatoes are golden.

Serves 4

Nutritional Analysis
per Serve

Total kJ: 1193

Total calories: 284

Carbohydrates: 25 g

Protein: 33 g

Fat – total: 4.9 g

Fat – saturated: 1.2 g

Fibre: 2.8 g

Salmon and broad bean patties

Get the kids to help you peel the broad beans. These patties are great served with Tomato and Mozzarella Salad (page 104).

1 cup frozen broad beans

400 g potatoes, boiled and peeled

1 x 210 g can red salmon, drained, bones removed and flaked

1 egg, lightly beaten

1 bunch chives, snipped

¼ cup grated low-fat cheese

salt and pepper

¾ cup fresh breadcrumbs

olive oil spray

Nutritional Analysis per Serve

Total kJ: 1067

Total calories: 254

Carbohydrates: 22 g

Protein: 18.6 g

Fat – total: 8.7 g

Fat – saturated: 2.9 g

Fibre: 5.9 g

- Preheat the oven to 180°C. Line an oven tray with baking paper.
- Place the broad beans in a large mixing bowl and cover with boiling water. Set aside for 5 minutes. Drain and peel the broad beans. Return the peeled beans to the bowl, add the cooked potatoes and mash together lightly.
- Add the flaked salmon, egg, chives and cheese to the bowl and mix well. Season to taste with salt and pepper. Use wet hands to shape the mixture into 8 patties. Coat each patty in breadcrumbs and place on the prepared oven tray.
- Spray the patties lightly with oil and bake in the oven for 10 minutes. Turn the patties and bake for a further 10 minutes.

Makes 8

Tandoori chicken skewers with yoghurt mint sauce

Tandoori pastes vary in fat content from brand to brand. Check the nutritional information when making your purchase and be sure to choose the one with the lowest fat and energy content. For this recipe you'll need 16 bamboo skewers, soaked in water for 30 minutes before grilling.

500 g chicken tenderloins

¼ cup tandoori paste

¼ cup Light & Creamy Coconut Flavoured Evaporated Milk

200 g low-fat natural yoghurt

2 tablespoons chopped mint leaves

1 tablespoon lemon juice

½ teaspoon sumac, plus extra to serve

2 cups steamed rice, to serve

Nutritional Analysis
per Serve

Total kJ: 1663

Total calories: 396

Carbohydrates: 32.3 g

Protein: 38 g

Fat – total: 12 g

Fat – saturated: 2.9 g

Fibre: 1.5 g

- Thread the chicken tenderloin pieces onto the prepared skewers and place in a shallow dish. Mix together the tandoori paste and evaporated milk and pour over the chicken. Turn to coat. Cover with plastic wrap and refrigerate for 2 hours to marinate.
- Meanwhile, place the yoghurt, mint, lemon juice and sumac in a bowl and mix well.
- Heat a non-stick frying pan over a medium heat. Cook the chicken skewers for 3 minutes on each side, basting regularly with the marinade, until browned and cooked through.
- Sprinkle the tandoori chicken skewers with a little extra sumac and serve with the yoghurt sauce and steamed rice.

Serves 4

Chicken and rocket kofta

Kofta are oval-shaped meatballs from the Middle East. They are usually made from minced lamb or beef, but minced chicken is just as delicious. Serve the kofta with Snow Pea Sprout and Herb Salad (page 96).

400 g lean chicken mince

50 g rocket, trimmed and finely chopped

1/2 cup couscous

2 cloves garlic, crushed

1/2 teaspoon paprika

1 egg, lightly beaten

salt and pepper

- Preheat the oven to 180°C. Line an oven tray with baking paper.
- Combine the chicken mince, rocket, couscous, garlic, paprika and egg in a bowl and mix well. Season with salt and pepper. Using wet hands, shape the mixture into 8 small oval patties and place on the prepared oven tray. Refrigerate for 10 minutes.
- Bake the kofta for 20 minutes, or until they are golden and cooked through.

Serves 4

Nutritional Analysis
per Serve

Total kJ: 916
Total calories: 218
Carbohydrates: 10 g
Protein: 22.8 g
Fat – total: 9.6 g
Fat – saturated: 2.8 g
Fibre: 0.6 g

Risotto with chicken and mushrooms

With our very busy lives it can be hard to find the time to make risotto the traditional way. With this baked risotto, you can still enjoy a family favourite without all of the stirring.

1½ cups arborio rice

1 leek, thinly sliced

1 teaspoon thyme leaves

3 cups hot chicken stock (page 61)

1 teaspoon olive oil

2 skinless chicken breast fillets, sliced thinly

250 g button mushrooms, sliced

2 tablespoons grated parmesan cheese

- Preheat the oven to 180°C.
- Combine the rice, leek and thyme in a 3-litre baking dish. Pour on the hot stock and stir. Cover with foil and bake for 25–30 minutes, until the rice is tender.
- Meanwhile, heat the oil in a non-stick frying pan over a high heat. Cook the chicken, stirring occasionally, for 5 minutes, or until cooked through. Add the mushrooms and cook for another 3 minutes. Add to the risotto with the parmesan cheese and mix well. Cover with foil and set aside for 5 minutes before serving.

Serves 4

Nutritional Analysis
per Serve

Total kJ: 2541
Total calories: 605
Carbohydrates: 64 g
Protein: 51 g
Fat – total: 15 g
Fat – saturated: 4.6 g
Fibre: 2.8 g

Chicken san choy bau

A quick and easy dish to prepare that is great for entertaining. Fried noodles are 5 cm lengths of precooked thin noodles, found in the Asian section of the supermarket.

olive oil spray

2 teaspoons grated ginger

2 onions, finely diced

4 cloves garlic, crushed

1 small red chilli, seeded and
   finely sliced

350 g chicken mince

1 teaspoon cornflour

1 egg yolk

4 iceberg lettuce leaf cups, washed

1 teaspoon sesame oil

1 teaspoon fish sauce

2 tablespoons lime juice

2 tablespoons light soy sauce

2 teaspoons kecap manis
   (sweet soy sauce)

¼ cup fried shallots

¼ cup fried noodles

¼ cup coriander leaves

¼ cup Vietnamese mint leaves

- Heat a large frying pan or wok over a low heat, spray lightly with oil and cook ginger, onions, garlic and chilli gently until soft. Increase the heat, add chicken mince and cook for a few minutes, breaking up with a wooden spoon.

- Combine cornflour and egg yolk to form a smooth paste.

- Drain off any excess liquid from the mince before adding the sesame oil, fish sauce, lime juice, soy sauce, kecap manis and egg mixture. Cook for 5 minutes over a medium heat, stirring occasionally, then remove from heat and mix through the fried shallots and noodles.

- Divide mixture evenly between the lettuce cups and top with coriander and mint leaves.

Serves 4

Nutritional Analysis
per Serve

Total kJ: 1107

Total calories: 266

Carbohydrates: 9 g

Protein: 27.9 g

Fat – total: 11.9 g

Fat – saturated: 3.3 g

Fibre: 3.5 g

Chicken and cashew stir-fry

Tender chicken, crunchy vegetables and cashews make this stir-fry a winner.

MARINADE

1 tablespoon grated ginger

½ small red chilli, seeded and finely sliced

2 cloves garlic, crushed

1 tablespoon soy sauce

1 teaspoon kecap manis (sweet soy sauce)

½ teaspoon fish sauce

1 tablespoon lime juice

½ teaspoon oyster sauce

½ teaspoon mirin (Japanese rice wine)

2 medium skinless chicken breasts, cut
    into 1 cm strips

olive oil spray

2 onions, finely sliced

1 tablespoon grated ginger

4 cloves garlic, crushed

120 g baby corn spears, cut into thirds

1 large head broccoli, cut into small florets

½ red capsicum, finely sliced

¼ cup water

100 g rice vermicelli noodles

1 teaspoon cornflour

7 water chestnuts, sliced

¼ cup raw cashews, roughly chopped

¼ cup chopped coriander leaves

- Combine marinade ingredients and pour half over the chicken. Marinate for 2 hours.
- Heat a wok or large frying pan over a low heat, spray lightly with oil, add the onions and cook until soft. Add ginger, garlic and corn and cook for 2 minutes. Remove chicken from marinade, reserving any liquid, and add to wok. Increase heat and toss until browned. Add broccoli, capsicum and water. Reduce to a simmer and cook for 7 minutes until tender. Stir through remaining marinade.
- Cover noodles with boiling water, stand for 2 minutes, then drain. Mix the cornflour with a teaspoon of water. Move all ingredients to one side of the wok and add cornflour mixture, stirring until it thickens. Add noodles, water chestnuts, cashews and coriander, mix thoroughly and serve.

Serves 4

Nutritional Analysis
per Serve

Total kJ: 1816
Total calories: 436
Carbohydrates: 17.6 g
Protein: 46.9 g
Fat – total: 18.3 g
Fat – saturated: 4.4 g
Fibre: 4.6 g

Herb-crusted grilled pork

This dish is perfect for barbecues and goes well with Fennel and Orange Salad (page 88).

1 teaspoon coriander seeds

2 teaspoons fennel seeds

1 teaspoon cumin seeds

freshly ground black pepper

rind of 2 oranges, grated

4 x 200 g pork mid-loin chops,
  trimmed

Nutritional Analysis
per Serve

Total kJ: 1300

Total calories: 312

Carbohydrates: 0 g

Fat – total: 20 g

Fat – saturated: 7.9 g

Protein: 32.8 g

Fibre: 0 g

- Using a mortar and pestle, crush the coriander, fennel and cumin seeds. If you prefer, use the same quantities of ground seeds.
- Mix the spices and orange rind. Roll the edges of the pork chops in the spice mix to coat evenly. Cook under a hot grill for 5-7 minutes on either side until golden brown.
- Rest in a warm place for 5 minutes, loosely covered with foil, before serving.

Serves 4

Cajun pork fillet with chargrilled salsa

Cajun seasoning mix is made from a blend of black pepper, cayenne pepper, chilli, mustard and paprika. Needless to say it has quite a kick to it, so decrease the amount to make this dish child-friendly.

1 x 500 g pork fillet

2 tablespoons Cajun seasoning mix

olive oil spray

2 corn cobs

2 tomatoes, diced

1 Lebanese cucumber, seeded and diced

¼ cup coriander leaves

2 lemons, halved

Nutritional Analysis
per Serve

Total kJ: 890
Total calories: 212
Carbohydrates: 10.6 g
Protein: 29.8 g
Fat – total: 4 g
Fat – saturated: 1 g
Fibre: 3.5 g

- Place the pork in a shallow dish and sprinkle Cajun seasoning mix all over to coat.

- Preheat a chargrill or barbecue over a medium heat and spray with oil. Cook the corn cobs for 10–12 minutes, turning frequently, until tender. Use a sharp knife to slice the kernels from each cob and place in a mixing bowl with the tomatoes, cucumber and coriander leaves.

- Spray the chargrill with a little more oil and cook the pork for 3–4 minutes on each side, or until cooked through. Rest for 5 minutes before slicing. Cook the lemon halves on the chargrill for 2 minutes, turning frequently, until lightly caramelised. Serve the pork with lemon halves and the chargrilled salsa.

Serves 4

Pork and veal meatballs with spaghetti

The combination of pork and veal makes these meatballs wonderfully full of flavour.

400 g pork and veal mince, combined
   weight

1 carrot, grated

½ cup fresh breadcrumbs

1 egg, lightly beaten

1 tablespoon snipped chives

2 teaspoons Worcestershire sauce

2 teaspoons mustard

salt and pepper

300 g spaghetti

olive oil spray

1 onion, chopped

2 cloves garlic, crushed

2 x 400 g cans reduced-salt
   chopped tomatoes

1 cup water

½ cup basil leaves

- Preheat the oven to 180°C. Line an oven tray with baking paper. Combine the pork and veal mince, carrot, breadcrumbs, egg, chives, Worcestershire sauce and mustard in a large mixing bowl. Season to taste and mix well. Using wet hands, roll tablespoons of mixture into balls. Place the meatballs on the prepared oven tray and bake for 20 minutes, until browned.

- Cook the spaghetti in a large saucepan of boiling water according to the packet instructions. Drain well.

- Meanwhile, heat a large saucepan over a medium heat. Spray with oil and cook the onion for 5 minutes, or until soft. Add the garlic and cook for a further minute. Stir in the tomatoes, water and basil and simmer for 10 minutes. Season well with salt and pepper. Add the meatballs to the tomato sauce and simmer for another 5 minutes. Divide the spaghetti between 4 serving bowls and top with the meatballs and sauce.

Serves 4

Nutritional Analysis
per Serve

Total kJ: 2138
Total calories: 509
Carbohydrates: 60 g
Protein: 35.2 g
Fat – total: 11.3 g
Fat – saturated: 3.5 g
Fibre: 11.4 g

Spice-crusted lamb fillet
with spinach and fetta salad

If the kids aren't big fans of spicy flavours, simply omit the chilli and cayenne pepper.

2 teaspoons ground coriander

1 teaspoon ground cumin

1/2 teaspoon chilli flakes

1/4 teaspoon cayenne pepper

3 lamb fillets (about 300 g in total)

olive oil spray

SALAD

100 g baby spinach leaves

1 punnet grape tomatoes, halved

1/2 small red onion, finely sliced

50 g low-fat fetta cheese, crumbled

1 tablespoon lemon juice

1 tablespoon chopped basil leaves

1 teaspoon extra-virgin olive oil

1 teaspoon Dijon mustard

- Mix together the spices and sprinkle on the lamb fillets to coat.
- Spray a non-stick frying pan with oil and heat on high. Cook the lamb for 3 minutes on each side for rare, and an extra 2 minutes on each side for medium. Cover loosely with foil and rest for 10 minutes.
- Place the spinach, tomato halves, onion and feta in a salad bowl. Mix together the lemon juice, basil, oil and mustard and toss through the salad. Slice the lamb diagonally into strips and serve with the salad.

Serves 4

Nutritional Analysis
per Serve

Total kJ: 790
Total calories: 188
Carbohydrates: 1.4 g
Protein: 16.8 g
Fat – total: 12.8 g
Fat – saturated: 6.5 g
Fibre: 1.4 g

Lemon and oregano pork loin with zucchini mash

The combination of lemon and oregano is often used in Greek-style marinades for lamb or chicken, but it is equally nice here with pork.

4 x 70 g pork loin steaks, trimmed of fat

1 tablespoon lemon juice

finely grated zest of 1 lemon

2 cloves garlic, crushed

1 teaspoon dried oregano leaves

3 medium potatoes, peeled and quartered

3 medium zucchini, chopped

¼ cup hot no-fat milk

salt and pepper

Nutritional Analysis
per Serve

Total kJ: 895

Total calories: 213

Carbohydrates: 17 g

Protein: 22 g

Fat – total: 5.1 g

Fat – saturated: 1.6 g

Fibre: 3.7 g

- Place the pork steaks in a shallow dish. Mix together the lemon juice and zest, garlic and oregano and pour over the pork steaks. Turn to coat. Cover with plastic wrap and refrigerate for 1 hour to marinate.
- Cook the potatoes in a large pan of boiling, salted water for 10 minutes. Add the zucchini and cook for a further 5 minutes. Drain and mash well with the hot milk. Season to taste.
- Heat a non-stick frying pan over a medium heat. Cook the pork steaks, basting frequently with marinade, for 3 minutes on each side, or until cooked to your liking.
- Drizzle over any juices from the pan and serve with the zucchini mash.

Serves 4

Lamb and bean casserole

A one pot, slow-cooking meal that melts in the mouth.

olive oil spray

300 g lean lamb, cubed

1 teaspoon olive oil

1 onion, chopped

2 cloves garlic, crushed

2 sticks celery, diced

2 medium potatoes, peeled and diced

2 carrots, diced

1 x 400 g can reduced-salt
  chopped tomatoes

¼ cup reduced-salt tomato paste

2 cups water

1 bay leaf

200 g canned borlotti beans, rinsed
  and drained

¼ cup chopped parsley leaves, to serve

- Preheat the oven to 180°C.
- Heat a large, flameproof casserole pan over a high heat and spray with oil. Brown the lamb cubes in batches and set aside. Heat the olive oil in the same pan over a medium heat. Cook the onion, garlic, celery, potato and carrot for 5 minutes. Return the lamb cubes to the pan with the tomatoes, tomato paste, water and bay leaf. Bring to the boil. Cover the pan, transfer to the oven and bake for 1 hour.
- Stir in the borlotti beans and cook for a further hour, stirring occasionally. Serve in deep bowls sprinkled with parsley.

VARIATION
- Nutritional analysis based on recipe using 1 medium zucchini and 1 leek instead of 2 potatoes and omitting the borlotti beans.

Serves 4

Nutritional Analysis
per Serve

Total kJ: 1168
Total calories: 278
Carbohydrates: 29.8 g
Protein: 17 g
Fat – total: 9 g
Fat – saturated: 4 g
Fibre: 6.7 g

Nutritional Analysis
per Serve

Total kJ: 739
Total calories: 176
Carbohydrates: 9.9 g
Protein: 12.1 g
Fat – total: 8.8 g
Fat – saturated: 4 g
Fibre: 5 g

Parsley, ricotta and garlic stuffed lamb

Lamb backstraps are also known as lamb loins. They are well known for being low in fat but very tender and flavourful.

½ cup low-fat ricotta
¼ cup chopped parsley leaves
2 cloves garlic, crushed
finely grated zest of 1 lemon
2 teaspoons lemon juice
salt and pepper
1 x 500 g lamb backstrap

- Combine the ricotta, parsley, garlic, lemon zest and juice and season well with salt and pepper. Cut the lamb fillet lengthways, halfway through to the centre. Open out and spread with ricotta stuffing. Tie the fillet with kitchen twine to seal.
- Heat a non-stick frying pan over a high heat. Cook the lamb for 5 minutes on each side until well browned. Remove from the heat, cover loosely with foil and set aside to rest for 10 minutes before slicing.

Serves 4

Nutritional Analysis
per Serve

Total kJ: 886
Total calories: 211
Carbohydrates: 1 g
Protein: 19 g
Fat – total: 14.6 g
Fat – saturated: 8.1 g
Fibre: 0.5 g

Yoghurt-marinated lamb cutlets

These cutlets, done on the barbecue and served with Tabbouleh (page 86), are the perfect summer meal.

¼ cup low-fat natural yoghurt

4 tablespoons finely shredded mint leaves

1 teaspoon dried mint

2 cloves garlic, crushed

½ teaspoon ground cumin

¼ teaspoon freshly ground black pepper

olive oil spray

12 lamb cutlets, trimmed

- Mix the yoghurt, mint, garlic, cumin and pepper together. Toss the cutlets through the mix until evenly coated. Marinate overnight or for a minimum of 5 hours.
- Heat a large frying pan over a medium heat and spray lightly with oil. (The cutlets can also be cooked under a hot grill or on the barbecue.) Cook for 5-8 minutes on each side. Cooking time will vary depending upon the thickness of the cutlets. Rest for 5 minutes, loosely covered with foil, before serving.

Serves 4

Nutritional Analysis
per Serve

Total kJ: 1152
Total calories: 276
Carbohydrates: 3.8 g
Protein: 36.9 g
Fat – total: 12.9 g
Fat – saturated: 6.8 g
Fibre: 0.4 g

Braised lamb shanks with lentil stew

When buying shanks, ask your butcher to cut the tendon. This helps the meat to fall off the bone while cooking, making it more flavoursome and tender.

4 lamb shanks

2 tablespoons plain flour

olive oil spray

2 onions, finely diced

3 sticks celery, finely diced

2 carrots, scraped and finely diced

4 sprigs thyme

3 tablespoons tomato paste

1/2 cup red wine

3 cups chicken stock (page 61)

1/2 cup brown lentils, rinsed

1 head garlic, cut in half widthwise

8 shallots, peeled

freshly ground black pepper

- Preheat oven to 180°C.
- Coat the shanks with flour. Heat a large frying pan over a high heat and spray lightly with oil. Brown shanks on all sides then remove. Add more oil if necessary, lower heat and cook the onions, celery, carrots and thyme gently for a few minutes until soft. Add tomato paste and cook for 2 minutes. Add the red wine and reduce for a further 2 minutes, then add the chicken stock and the shanks. Increase heat and bring to the boil. Transfer the contents of the pan to a deep baking dish. Add lentils, garlic and shallots, cover with a lid or foil and bake for 2 hours, turning the shanks every 30 minutes.
- Remove the foil and cook for a further 30 minutes until meat is falling off the bone. Remove the shanks and keep warm. Skim any fat from the surface of the liquid, remove the thyme and pour into a saucepan. Bring to the boil then turn down the heat and cook for 7-10 minutes or until thick. Return the shanks to the pan, season with pepper and serve.

Nutritional Analysis
per Serve

Total kJ: 1284

Total calories: 308

Carbohydrates: 11.8 g

Protein: 36 g

Fat – total: 11 g

Fat – saturated: 5.5 g

Fibre: 4.2 g

Serves 4

Steak sandwich

If you can't find minute steaks use tenderised rump steaks instead.

olive oil spray

150 g cherry tomatoes, halved

100 g mushrooms, wiped and chopped

4 x 150 g minute steaks

125 g lettuce leaves

1 red onion, finely sliced

4 slices sourdough bread

2 tablespoons horseradish cream

freshly ground black pepper

- Heat a large frying pan over a medium heat and spray lightly with oil. Place the tomatoes and mushrooms in the pan and cook gently for a couple of minutes. Remove the tomatoes and put them in a warm place. Move mushrooms to one side of the frying pan and add the steaks. Cook for 2-4 minutes on each side.
- Arrange the lettuce, onion, tomatoes and mushrooms on unbuttered slices of toasted sourdough and finish with a dollop of horseradish cream and pepper to taste. Serve immediately.

Serves 4

Nutritional Analysis
per Serve

Total kJ: 1032

Total calories: 248

Carbohydrates: 16.6 g

Protein: 23.2 g

Fat – total: 8.9 g

Fat – saturated: 3.6 g

Fibre: 3.5 g

Spiced vegetable ratatouille with couscous

Freeze any excess spice mix and sprinkle onto roasted vegetables for flavour.

SPICE MIX

1 teaspoon cayenne pepper

1 teaspoon freshly ground black pepper

1½ teaspoons sweet paprika

1½ teaspoons ground ginger

1 tablespoon ground turmeric

2 teaspoons ground cinnamon

2 teaspoons ground cumin

1 teaspoon allspice

¼ teaspoon sea salt

¼ butternut pumpkin, peeled, seeded
    and cut into 2 cm pieces

1 carrot, scraped and diced

½ eggplant, diced

olive oil spray

2 red onions, diced

2 sticks celery, diced

1 zucchini, diced

3 cloves garlic, crushed

1 x 400 g can chickpeas,
    rinsed and drained

2 cups tomato passata

2 cups water

juice of ½ lemon

1 cup couscous

1 tablespoon unsalted butter

1 cup boiling water

- Preheat oven to 220°C
- Combine all spice mix ingredients. Arrange pumpkin, carrot and eggplant on a baking tray, spray lightly with oil and sprinkle with 1 tablespoon of spice mix. Bake for 30 minutes until tender.
- Heat a large saucepan over a low heat and spray lightly with oil. Cook the onion and celery until soft, add the zucchini, garlic and 1 teaspoon of spice mix, and cook for 2 minutes. Add the chickpeas, vegetables, tomato passata and water. Cover and simmer over a low heat for 40 minutes until all vegetables are soft. When cooked add lemon juice and more spice mix to taste.
- Combine couscous, butter and boiling water in a bowl. Cover and let stand for 5 minutes, then loosen the grains with a fork. To serve place the couscous in a large bowl and arrange the vegetables on top.

Serves 6

Nutritional Analysis
per Serve

Total kJ: 1028
Total calories: 247
Carbohydrates: 32.8 g
Protein: 10 g
Fat – total: 6 g
Fat – saturated: 2.8 g
Fibre: 9 g

Grilled eye fillet with mustard polenta

Polenta is derived from corn so is great for those on a gluten-free diet.

2 tomatoes, cut in half widthwise
olive oil spray
2 teaspoons chopped oregano leaves
freshly ground black pepper
4 x 200 g eye fillet steaks

POLENTA
2 cups water
1$\frac{1}{2}$ cups low-fat milk
$\frac{2}{3}$ cup polenta
1$\frac{1}{2}$ teaspoons hot English mustard
1$\frac{1}{2}$ tablespoons seeded mustard

Nutritional Analysis
per Serve

Total kJ: 1158
Total calories: 278
Carbohydrates: 3.9 g
Protein: 39 g
Fat - total: 11.3 g
Fat - saturated: 5.2 g
Fibre: 0.8 g

- Preheat oven to 150°C.
- Place tomatoes on a baking tray and spray lightly with oil. Top with oregano leaves and pepper. Bake in the oven for 30-40 minutes until tender.
- Bring water and milk to the boil in a saucepan over a medium heat. Whisk in the polenta, ensuring it is well combined. Reduce heat and simmer for 40 minutes, whisking occasionally, until smooth and thick.
- Halfway through the polenta cooking time, cook steaks under a hot grill for 5-7 minutes on each side. Alternatively, heat a large frying pan over a high heat and spray lightly with oil. Cook the steaks for 5-7 minutes on each side or as desired.
- Set steaks aside to rest for 5 minutes in a warm place, loosely covered with foil. Add the mustards to the polenta and mix well. Spoon polenta onto each plate and place steak on top. Drizzle over any juices from the pan and serve with the roasted tomatoes.

Serves 4

Thai beef salad

A light and satisfying meal with lots of flavour.

MARINADE

2½ teaspoons oyster sauce

½ teaspoon sesame oil

⅓ cup mirin (Japanese rice wine)

½ small red chilli, seeded and finely
  sliced

1 tablespoon grated ginger

2 cloves garlic, crushed

500 g rump steak, trimmed

olive oil spray

1 cup torn Vietnamese mint leaves

1 cup torn basil leaves

½ cup chopped coriander leaves

1½ teaspoons sesame seeds

4 spring onions, finely sliced

1 cup fried noodles

8 mango cheeks (roughly half a 425 g
  can), drained and cut into 1 cm slices,
  reserving 3 tablespoons juice

2 small red chillies, seeded and finely
  sliced

2 tablespoons fried shallots

10 cherry tomatoes, halved

DRESSING

1½ tablespoons soy sauce

3 tablespoons lime juice

2 cloves garlic, crushed

1½ teaspoons grated ginger

2 teaspoons mirin (Japanese rice wine)

3 tablespoons reserved mango juice

½ teaspoon sesame oil

1 tablespoon oyster sauce

- Combine marinade ingredients and pour
  over beef, tossing to coat. Marinate
  overnight or for a minimum of 4 hours.
- Heat a frying pan over a high heat and
  spray lightly with oil. Cook the steaks for
  3-5 minutes on each side, then remove
  from the pan and allow to cool slightly.
- Combine salad ingredients. To make dressing
  place all ingredients in an airtight jar and
  shake to combine. Slice beef diagonally into
  1 cm strips, add to salad
  and drizzle with
  dressing.

Serves 4

Nutritional Analysis
per Serve

Total kJ: 1397
Total calories: 335
Carbohydrates: 15.2 g
Protein: 30.4 g
Fat - total: 13.6 g
Fat - saturated: 5.4 g
Fibre: 4.1 g

Chermoula-crusted beef
with chickpea and tomato salad

Chermoula is a North African spice mix with a delightful lemony flavour. The chopped skin of a preserved lemon is traditionally used but grated lemon rind is a suitable substitute.

200 g canned chickpeas, rinsed and
   drained
½ small red onion, sliced
200 g grape tomatoes, quartered
2 tablespoons lemon juice
olive oil spray
4 x 100 g pieces sirloin steak

CHERMOULA
2 tablespoons parsley leaves
2 tablespoons mint leaves
2 tablespoons coriander leaves
2 teaspoons ground cumin
2 teaspoons ground coriander
1 teaspoon sumac
1 teaspoon ground black pepper
1 tablespoon chopped preserved lemon
   rind or finely grated lemon rind
¼ cup water
½ small red onion, chopped

- To make the chermoula, place all the ingredients in the bowl of a small food processor. Pulse until the mixture forms a paste.
- Meanwhile, combine the chickpeas, onion, tomatoes and lemon juice in a mixing bowl and toss to combine.
- Heat a large, non-stick frying pan over a high heat and spray with oil. Cook the steaks for 4 minutes, then turn them and baste with chermoula on the cooked side. Cook for a further 3 minutes, or until cooked to your liking.
- Set the steaks aside to rest for a few minutes in a warm place. Serve with the chickpea and tomato salad.

Serves 4

Nutritional Analysis
per Serve

Total kJ: 865
Total calories: 206
Carbohydrates: 8.7 g
Protein: 24 g
Fat – total: 7.4 g
Fat – saturated: 2.9 g
Fibre: 3.7 g

Beef and mushroom stroganoff

Stroganoff is a traditional Russian dish. Use low-fat natural yoghurt in place of the sour cream if you prefer.

1 teaspoon olive oil

400 g topside steak, cut into strips

1 onion, halved and sliced

2 cloves garlic, crushed

1 teaspoon smoked paprika

250 g button mushrooms, sliced

1 cup reduced-salt beef stock

2 tablespoons tomato paste

1/2 cup extra-light sour cream

200 g cooked noodles, to serve

1/4 cup chopped parsley leaves, to serve

- Heat the oil in a large non-stick frying pan over a high heat. Brown the steak strips in batches and set aside. Reduce the heat to medium, add the onion and cook for 5 minutes, until tender. Add the garlic and paprika and stir for 1 minute, until fragrant.
- Return the beef to the pan with the mushrooms, stock and tomato paste. Bring to the boil, then reduce the heat to low and simmer for 10 minutes. Remove the pan from the heat and stir in the sour cream.
- Serve the stroganoff with the noodles and sprinkle with chopped parsley.

Serves 4

Nutritional Analysis
per Serve

Total kJ: 1210

Total calories: 288

Carbohydrates: 19.4 g

Protein: 27.4 g

Fat – total: 10.2 g

Fat – saturated: 4.8 g

Fibre: 3.5 g

Stir-fried beef and bok choy in oyster sauce

There are a number of different types of bok choy, which is also known as pak choy. For this recipe we like to use baby bok choy.

1 teaspoon rice bran oil

1 onion, halved and sliced

2 cloves garlic, crushed

1 teaspoon grated ginger

400 g lean beef strips

1 bunch bok choy, leaves separated and washed

¼ cup reduced-salt beef stock

¼ cup oyster sauce

2 cups steamed rice, to serve

- Heat the oil in a wok or large frying pan over a high heat. Cook the onion for 3 minutes, or until tender. Add the garlic and ginger and stir-fry for 1 minute until fragrant. Add the beef strips and cook for 3 minutes, or until brown. Add the bok choy, stock and oyster sauce to the wok and simmer for 3 minutes, or until the bok choy has wilted slightly.
- Serve with steamed rice.

Serves 4

Nutritional Analysis per Serve

Total kJ: 1184

Total calories: 282

Carbohydrates: 29.5 g

Protein: 24.4 g

Fat - total: 6.6 g

Fat - saturated: 2.3 g

Fibre: 1.5 g

Tomato chilli prawns

This recipe shows how quick and easy it is to prepare delicious, healthy food.

1 teaspoon olive oil

1 onion, chopped

5 cloves garlic, crushed

1 small red chilli, finely chopped

1 x 400 g can chopped tomatoes

2 tablespoons tomato paste

finely grated zest and juice of 1 lime

½ teaspoon sugar

½ cup water

salt and pepper

1 kg green (raw) prawns, peeled and
    deveined, tails intact

½ cup chopped coriander leaves

2 cups steamed rice, to serve

- Heat the oil in a frying pan over a medium heat. Cook the onion for 5 minutes, or until tender. Add the garlic and chilli and cook for 1 minute, until fragrant. Add the tomatoes, tomato paste, lime zest and juice, sugar and water. Season well with salt and pepper and simmer for 5 minutes.
- Add the prawns and coriander and simmer for 3 minutes, or until the prawns are pink and firm. Serve with steamed rice.

Serves 4

Nutritional Analysis
per Serve

Total kJ: 1663
Total calories: 396
Carbohydrates: 33 g
Protein: 55 g
Fat – total: 3.2 g
Fat – saturated: 0.5 g
Fibre: 3 g

Steak with horseradish sauce

Horseradish is a spicy root from the mustard family that goes beautifully with beef. If you use fresh horseradish, simply peel and grate it finely. Creamed horseradish is readily available in jars from the supermarket.

¼ cup low-fat natural yoghurt

1 teaspoon horseradish

olive oil spray

4 x 100 g pieces scotch fillet

2 bunches asparagus, trimmed

4 roma tomatoes, halved

4 pattypan squash, halved

Nutritional Analysis
per Serve

Total kJ: 722
Total calories: 172
Carbohydrates: 4.6 g
Protein: 25 g
Fat – total: 5.3 g
Fat – saturated: 2.3 g
Fibre: 2.5 g

- Combine the yoghurt and horseradish in a small bowl. Cover and refrigerate until ready to use.
- Heat a chargrill over a high heat and spray with oil. Cook the steaks for 3 minutes on each side for rare and an extra 5 minutes for well done. Remove from the heat, cover loosely with foil and set aside in a warm place to rest for 5 minutes.
- Meanwhile, spray the vegetables with oil and cook on the chargrill for about 5 minutes, turning occasionally.
- Serve the steak with the chargrilled vegetables and a dollop of horseradish sauce.

Serves 4

Desserts and sweet treats

Berry and mint sorbet

A light, fruity dessert that is perfect on hot summer days.

½ cup caster sugar

1½ cups water

¾ cup mixed berries

½ cup roughly chopped mint leaves

extra mint leaves to garnish

Nutritional Analysis
per Serve

Total kJ: 534

Total calories: 128

Carbohydrates: 32 g

Protein: 0.6 g

Fat – total: 0 g

Fat – saturated: 0 g

Fibre: 1 g

- Heat sugar and water in a saucepan, stirring occasionally until sugar dissolves. Bring to the boil over a medium heat, add berries and cook for a couple of minutes until soft. Remove from the heat, add the mint leaves and allow to cool completely.
- Strain the mixture through a sieve to remove all the berry seeds and pour into a plastic container. Freeze overnight.

Serves 4

Blood orange jelly

Blood oranges are in season from July to early September. At other times of the year use the juice from navel or Valencia oranges.

2 cups freshly squeezed blood orange
   juice
¼ cup caster sugar
1 tablespoon gelatine powder
¼ cup hot water
2 oranges, segmented, to serve

Nutritional Analysis
per Serve

Total kJ: 550
Total calories: 131
Carbohydrates: 28 g
Protein: 4.1 g
Fat – total: 0 g
Fat – saturated: 0 g
Fibre: 1.6 g

- Place the blood orange juice and sugar in a saucepan over a medium heat. Stir until the sugar has dissolved, then simmer for 3 minutes.
- Whisk together the gelatine and hot water until the gelatine has dissolved. Pour into the hot juice and stir to combine. Pour into four ½-cup moulds or two 1-cup jelly moulds and refrigerate overnight to set.
- To serve, dip each mould into warm water for 20 seconds to loosen the jellies and invert onto serving plates. Serve with orange segments.

Serves 4

Passionfruit soufflés

Low in fat and so easy to make!

10 passionfruit, or ½ cup canned pulp,
    strained to remove seeds
olive oil spray
¾ cup caster sugar
5 egg whites

Nutritional Analysis
per Serve

Total kJ: 853
Total calories: 205
Carbohydrates: 42.5 g
Protein: 5.8 g
Fat - total: 0.1 g
Fat - saturated: 0 g
Fibre: 6.3 g

- Preheat oven to 200°C.
- If using fresh passionfruit, remove seeds and pulp. Pass half the amount through a seive, reserving juice and discarding seeds.
- Heat remaining seeds, juice and sugar in a saucepan over a low heat and cook, stirring, until thickened.
- Spray 4 individual (1-cup capacity) ramekins lightly with oil, then sprinkle with a small amount of caster sugar, ensuring that the base and sides are lightly coated.
- Whisk egg whites until they begin to thicken. Add the sugar slowly while whisking and continue until soft peaks form. Gently fold the passionfruit through, reserving a little of the syrup.
- Spoon mixture into ramekins, leaving 1 cm at the top. Bake in the oven for 15–20 minutes until the soufflés have risen and are golden brown.
- Drizzle with the reserved passionfruit syrup and serve.

Serves 4

Pear and coconut spring rolls

A sweet twist on an old favourite.

3 cups (650 g) canned pears

½ cup shredded coconut

½ cup wheatgerm

6 sheets filo pastry

olive oil spray

2 tablespoons brown sugar

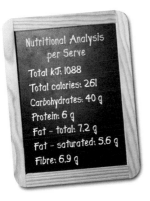

Nutritional Analysis
per Serve

Total kJ: 1088

Total calories: 261

Carbohydrates: 40 g

Protein: 6 g

Fat – total: 7.2 g

Fat – saturated: 5.6 g

Fibre: 6.9 g

- Place pears in a mixing bowl and combine with the coconut and wheatgerm.
- Place 1 sheet of filo on a flat surface, covering the others to prevent them drying out. Spray the sheet lightly with oil and fold in half. Spray lightly again and sprinkle over a small amount of the brown sugar.
- Spoon a sixth of the fruit mixture evenly along the bottom edge of the filo square and roll the square up tightly, spraying lightly with oil to finish and seal. Repeat for the remaining sheets.
- Heat a large frying pan over a medium heat and spray lightly with oil. Cut the spring rolls in half and cook for 2 minutes on each side until golden brown. Serve hot.

Serves 4

Pavlova roll

A deliciously light treat that everyone will enjoy.

4 egg whites
½ cup caster sugar
1 teaspoon cornflour
½ teaspoon white vinegar
icing sugar, for dusting
200 g low-fat vanilla fromage frais
250 g strawberries, hulled and halved

Nutritional Analysis
per Serve

Total kJ: 302
Total calories: 72
Carbohydrates: 14 g
Protein: 3.5 g
Fat – total: 0 g
Fat – saturated: 0 g
Fibre: 0.6 g

- Preheat the oven to 180°C. Line a 26 x 32 cm Swiss roll pan with baking paper.
- Using an electric mixer, beat the egg whites until soft peaks form. Add the sugar, 1 tablespoon at a time, until all the sugar is incorporated and the meringue is thick and glossy. Beat in the cornflour and vinegar. Spoon the meringue into the prepared pan, gently smoothing the surface with a metal spatula. Bake for 12–15 minutes until the surface is puffed and lightly golden.
- Turn the pavlova roll out onto a clean tea towel that has been lightly dusted with icing sugar. Peel away the baking paper and with the long side facing you, carefully roll up, using the tea towel as a guide. Set aside to cool.
- When the pavlova is completely cool, unroll it and spread with the fromage frais, leaving a 2 cm border around the edges. Top with the strawberries and re-roll. Slice and serve.

Serves 10

Vanilla-poached nashi pears

Also known as Asian pears, nashi have a crisp juicy flesh that is delicious eaten raw or poached.

2 vanilla beans

3 cups water

½ cup caster sugar

1 cinnamon stick

2 pieces of orange peel

4 nashi pears, peeled

Nutritional Analysis
per Serve

Total kJ: 752
Total calories: 179
Carbohydrates: 44 g
Protein: 0.7 g
Fat – total: 0.2 g
Fat – saturated: 0 g
Fibre: 2.6 g

- Use a sharp paring knife to split the vanilla beans lengthways and scrape out the seeds. Place seeds and split beans in a medium saucepan with the water, sugar, cinnamon and orange peel. Stir over a low heat until the sugar has dissolved.
- Add the nashi pears to the pan and increase the heat to medium. Simmer, covered, for 10 minutes, or until the nashi pears are tender. Remove the pan from the heat and leave for 10 minutes for the flavours to infuse.
- Serve the poached nashi pears warm or cold, drizzled with syrup.

Serves 4

Individual raspberry trifles

We used low-fat lemon biscuits for this recipe, but there are plenty of other varieties available at your supermarket.

300 g low-fat vanilla yoghurt
1/2 cup low-fat pouring custard
4 low-fat lemon biscuits
4 meringue nests
250 g raspberries

- Place the yoghurt and custard in a bowl and mix until smooth. Roughly chop the biscuits and meringues together.
- Sprinkle a little of the combined biscuit and meringue mixture over the base of 4 serving glasses. Top with some raspberries and a dollop of the yoghurt mixture. Repeat the layers once more, finishing with raspberries. Refrigerate for 10 minutes before serving.

Serves 4

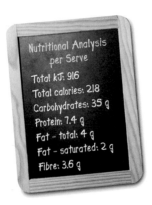

Nutritional Analysis
per Serve

Total kJ: 916
Total calories: 218
Carbohydrates: 35 g
Protein: 7.4 g
Fat - total: 4 g
Fat - saturated: 2 g
Fibre: 3.6 g

Fairy cup cakes

These are best eaten on the day they are made.

2 eggs

2 tablespoons caster sugar

½ cup self-raising flour, sifted

½ teaspoon baking powder

2 tablespoons extra-light spreadable
cream cheese

2 tablespoons low-fat custard

½ teaspoon caster sugar

½ teaspoon vanilla essence

¼ teaspoon cinnamon

icing sugar, for dusting

- Preheat the oven to 180°C. Line a 12-hole patty tin with paper cases.
- Using an electric mixer, beat the eggs and sugar until pale and creamy. Fold in the flour and baking powder until just combined. Spoon into the paper cases, until two-thirds full. Bake for 12–15 minutes, or until the cakes spring back when lightly pressed. Cool the cup cakes on a wire rack.
- Mix together the cream cheese, custard, sugar, vanilla and cinnamon until smooth. Cut a disc from the top of each cup cake and fill with the cream cheese mixture. Replace the top and repeat with the remaining cakes. Dust with icing sugar before serving.

Makes 12

Nutritional Analysis
per Cake

Total kJ: 227
Total calories: 54
Carbohydrates: 8 g
Protein: 2 g
Fat – total: 1.5 g
Fat – saturated: 0.7 g
Fibre: 0.2 g

Apple and rhubarb crumble

This oaty crumble is perfect on a cold winter's night.

4 cups Stewed Apple and Rhubarb
   (page 54)
3 tablespoons butter
$^1/_2$ cup rolled oats
$^1/_4$ cup shredded coconut
2 tablespoons almond meal
$^1/_4$ teaspoon cinnamon

Nutritional Analysis
per Serve

Total kJ: 1101
Total calories: 264
Carbohydrates: 11.3 g
Protein: 5.4 g
Fat – total: 19.5 g
Fat – saturated: 11.6 g
Fibre: 8.1 g

- Preheat oven to 180°C.
- Divide the stewed apple and rhubarb evenly between 4 individual (1-cup capacity) ramekins.
- Place the butter and half the oats in a food processor and process until the mixture is the consistency of breadcrumbs. Tip into a mixing bowl and add the rest of the oats, coconut, almond meal and cinnamon.
- Spoon the crumble mix over the fruit and bake for 15–20 minutes until crisp and golden.
- Remove from the oven and let stand for 5 minutes before serving. Delicious served with low-fat natural yoghurt.

Serves 4

Apricot, ginger and honey cookies

The kick of ginger makes these cookies extra special.

1 cup plain flour

1 cup rolled oats

1/2 teaspoon baking powder

2 tablespoons brown sugar

100 g butter

1/4 cup honey

rind of 1 orange, finely grated

1 egg

1/2 teaspoon vanilla essence

1/4 cup finely diced dried apricots

2 tablespoons finely diced crystallised
   ginger

- Preheat oven to 175°C.
- Mix together the flour, oats, baking powder and sugar. In a small saucepan gently melt the butter and honey. Remove from heat and add the orange rind, egg and vanilla essence. Pour over the oat mixture and combine, adding the apricots and ginger.
- Spoon onto a lined baking tray, leaving room between each. Press to flatten into 5 cm rounds, and bake in the oven for 20 minutes until golden brown.

Makes 18 cookies (3 per serve)

Nutritional Analysis
per Serve

Total kJ: 1494
Total calories: 359
Carbohydrates: 44 g
Protein: 6 g
Fat – total: 17 g
Fat – saturated: 9.6 g
Fibre: 4.1 g

Carrot, sultana and walnut muffins

Low in fat but high in flavour, these muffins make a great morning or afternoon snack.

1 cup wholemeal self-raising flour

¾ cup self-raising flour

⅓ cup brown sugar

1½ teaspoons ground cinnamon

¾ cup orange juice

2 tablespoons light sour cream

1 egg

½ cup finely grated carrot

⅓ cup sultanas

2 tablespoons chopped walnuts

- Preheat oven to 180°C.
- Mix both types of flour, sugar and cinnamon in a large bowl. In a separate bowl combine orange juice, sour cream and egg.
- Fold the mixture into the flour, add carrot, sultanas and walnuts and stir until well combined. Spoon into a greased muffin tin and bake for 20 minutes until golden and firm to the touch.

Makes 10 muffins

Nutritional Analysis
per Serve

Total kJ: 805

Total calories: 193

Carbohydrates: 33.2 g

Protein: 5.4 g

Fat – total: 3.3 g

Fat – saturated: 0.9 g

Fibre: 3.8 g

Apricot upside-down cake

Upside-down cakes are known for their moist texture, and this one certainly confirms that.

vegetable or canola oil spray

2 tablespoons low-joule apricot jam

1 x 410 g can unsweetened apricot halves, drained

2 eggs

1/2 cup caster sugar

3/4 cup Light & Creamy Evaporated Milk

1 teaspoon vanilla essence

1 1/2 cups self-raising flour, sifted

icing sugar, for dusting

Nutritional Analysis
per Serve

Total kJ: 458
Total calories: 109
Carbohydrates: 21 g
Protein: 3.7 g
Fat – total: 1 g
Fat – saturated: 0.4 g
Fibre: 1 g

- Preheat the oven to 180°C. Spray a 18 x 26 cm baking tray with oil and line the base with baking paper.
- Heat the jam in the microwave for 20 seconds on high and mix until smooth. Spread over the base of the prepared pan and top with the apricot halves.
- Using an electric mixer, beat the eggs and sugar until pale and creamy. Add the evaporated milk and vanilla and beat well. Fold in the flour and mix gently to combine. Pour into the prepared baking tray, being careful not to disturb the apricots. Bake for 35 minutes, or until cooked when tested with a skewer.
- Cool in the pan for 5 minutes before turning onto a serving plate. Dust with icing sugar before serving.

Serves 16

Chocolate mousse

When beating egg whites it is important to use a clean, dry bowl, as any moisture will prevent them from forming soft peaks.

2 egg whites

80 g dark chocolate, melted and cooled

400 g low-fat vanilla yoghurt

Nutritional Analysis
per Serve

Total kJ: 785
Total calories: 187
Carbohydrates: 23.6 g
Protein: 8.4 g
Fat – total: 6.3 g
Fat – saturated: 5.6 g
Fibre: 0.9 g

- Using an electric mixer, beat the egg whites until soft peaks form. Gradually add the chocolate, beating constantly until smooth and well combined. Fold in the yoghurt.
- Spoon into small serving bowls and refrigerate overnight to set.

Makes 4

Chocolate fudge cake

This cake is very moist and meringue-like. For a delicious dessert, try serving it with fresh berries.

60 g dark chocolate, finely chopped

¼ cup cocoa, plus extra for dusting

¼ cup boiling water

6 egg whites

¾ cup caster sugar

½ cup plain flour, sifted

Nutritional Analysis
per Serve

Total kJ: 412

Total calories: 98

Carbohydrates: 17.6 g

Protein: 2.9 g

Fat – total: 1.9 g

Fat – saturated: 1.6 g

Fibre: 0.5 g

- Preheat the oven to 170°C. Line the base and sides of a 20 cm springform cake tin with baking paper.
- Place the chocolate and cocoa in a small bowl. Pour on the boiling water and stir until the chocolate has melted and the mixture is smooth.
- Using an electric mixer, beat the egg whites until soft peaks form. Add the sugar, 1 tablespoon at a time, and continue beating until the sugar has completely dissolved and the meringue is thick and glossy. Add the chocolate mixture and mix to combine. Use a metal spoon to gently fold in the flour until just combined. Pour into the prepared tin and bake for 45 minutes, or until firm. Cool in the oven with the door ajar.
- Remove the cake from the tin and serve in wedges dusted with cocoa.

Serves 12

Dressings, sauces and toppings

Dressings

Herb mayonnaise

The beauty of this simple dressing is that you can use your favourite fresh herbs to achieve the flavour you want.

⅓ cup low-fat mayonnaise

2 teaspoons snipped chives

2 teaspoons chopped basil leaves

2 teaspoons chopped parsley leaves

· Place all the ingredients in an airtight jar and shake to combine. This dressing will keep in the refrigerator overnight.

Makes ⅓ cup

Nutritional Analysis
per Recipe

Total kJ: 743

Total calories: 177

Carbohydrates: 17 g

Protein: 0.6 g

Fat – total: 12 g

Fat – saturated: 2.6 g

Fibre: 0.9 g

Thousand island dressing

Great with seafood, this popular dressing can also be used in coleslaw.

⅓ cup low-fat mayonnaise

1 tablespoon tomato paste

1 teaspoon Worcestershire sauce

dash of Tabasco sauce

· Place all the ingredients in an airtight jar and shake to combine. This dressing will keep in the refrigerator for up to 1 week.

Makes ⅓ cup

Nutritional Analysis
per Recipe

Total kJ: 811

Total calories: 193

Carbohydrates: 20 g

Protein: 1.2 g

Fat – total: 11.8 g

Fat – saturated: 2.6 g

Fibre: 1.5 g

Chilli and lime dressing

This Asian-inspired dressing is delicious with oysters, Asian noodle salads or even as a dipping sauce for dumplings.

2 tablespoons lime juice

1 tablespoon fish sauce

2 teaspoons sugar

1 clove garlic, finely chopped

1 small red chilli, seeded and
    finely chopped

2 drops sesame oil

- Place all the ingredients in an airtight jar and shake to combine. This dressing will keep in the refrigerator overnight.

Makes ⅓ cup

Nutritional Analysis
per Recipe

Total kJ: 277
Total calories: 66
Carbohydrates: 9 g
Protein: 2.3 g
Fat – total: 1.4 g
Fat – saturated: 0.2 g
Fibre: 1 g

Mustard vinaigrette

A classic dressing that can be used on almost any salad.

2 tablespoons extra-virgin olive oil

1 tablespoon white wine vinegar

2 teaspoons Dijon mustard

salt and pepper

· Place all the ingredients in an airtight jar
  and shake to combine. This dressing will
  keep in the refrigerator overnight.

Makes ¼ cup

Nutritional Analysis
per Recipe

Total kJ: 1390
Total calories: 331
Carbohydrates: 0.2 g
Protein: 0.5 g
Fat – total: 37 g
Fat – saturated: 5.2 g
Fibre: 0.4 g

Sauces

Tartare sauce

The perfect accompaniment to seafood.

⅓ cup low-fat mayonnaise

1 gherkin, finely chopped

1 teaspoon chopped capers

· Mix all the ingredients together. Cover and refrigerate until ready to serve.

Makes ⅓ cup

Nutritional Analysis
per Recipe

Total kJ: 823
Total calories: 196
Carbohydrates: 21 g
Protein: 0.5 g
Fat – total: 11.7 g
Fat – saturated: 2.6 g
Fibre: 1 g

Low-fat white sauce

Try this low-fat version of white sauce in all your favourite recipes.

1 cup no-fat milk

2 teaspoons cornflour

2 tablespoons grated low-fat cheese

salt and pepper

Place the milk, cornflour and cheese in a small saucepan over a low heat. Season well with salt and pepper and stir until the mixture simmers and thickens slightly.

Makes 1 cup

Nutritional Analysis
per Recipe

Total kJ: 281
Total calories: 67
Carbohydrates: 6 g
Protein: 6 g
Fat – total: 2.5 g
Fat – saturated: 1.6 g
Fibre: 0 g

Dill tzatziki

Use this great sauce as an accompaniment to salmon patties, fish dishes and even lamb.

1 cup low-fat natural yoghurt

2 teaspoons lemon juice

1 clove garlic, crushed

2 tablespoons snipped dill

- Place all the ingredients in a mixing bowl and whisk gently to combine. Cover and refrigerate until ready to serve.

Makes 1 cup

Nutritional Analysis
per Recipe

Total kJ: 613

Total calories: 146

Carbohydrates: 15.7 g

Protein: 15.5 g

Fat – total: 0.6 g

Fat – saturated: 0.3 g

Fibre: 0.5 g

Toppings

Chocolate sauce

This chocolate sauce can be made several hours ahead. Simply reheat it gently before serving.

50 g dark chocolate, chopped

½ cup boiling water

2 tablespoons cocoa powder, sifted

1 tablespoon caster sugar, sifted

- Place the chocolate and half the boiling water in a small saucepan. Stir over a low heat until smooth. In a separate bowl, combine the cocoa powder and sugar with the remaining water to form a thick paste. Stir into the melted chocolate mixture.

Makes ²/₃ cup

Nutritional Analysis
per Recipe

Total kJ: 1530
Total calories: 366
Carbohydrates: 49 g
Protein: 5 g
Fat – total: 17 g
Fat – saturated: 15 g
Fibre: 3 g

Orange sauce

This sweet citrus sauce is delicious drizzled over grilled fruit or low-fat ice cream.

½ cup freshly squeezed orange juice

2 teaspoons caster sugar

1 teaspoon cornflour

1 teaspoon water

Nutritional Analysis
per Recipe

Total kJ: 256
Total calories: 61
Carbohydrates: 20 g
Protein: 0.7 g
Fat – total: 0.1 g
Fat – saturated: 0 g
Fibre: 0.3 g

· Place the orange juice and sugar in a small saucepan. Stir over a low heat until the sugar has dissolved. Mix the cornflour with a teaspoon of water to form a paste. Stir into the orange juice mixture and simmer until the sauce has thickened slightly. Serve hot or cold.

Makes ½ cup

Crumble topping

This recipe makes enough topping for a 4-person crumble. Use over any fruit combination.

⅓ cup natural (untoasted) muesli

1 tablespoon plain flour

1 tablespoon brown sugar

30 g low-fat spread

- Preheat the oven to 180°C.
- Combine the muesli, flour and sugar in a small bowl. Use your fingers to rub in the low-fat spread until well combined.
- Place the fruit of your choice in an ovenproof dish and cover with the crumble topping. Bake for 15–20 minutes, depending on the type of fruit you are using, until the topping is crisp and golden.

Makes ½ cup

Nutritional Analysis
per Recipe

Total kJ: 1411
Total calories: 336
Carbohydrates: 37 g
Protein: 4.5 g
Fat – total: 18 g
Fat – saturated: 3.6 g
Fibre: 4.8 g

Index